Faith and Finances

*A 21st Century Biblical Guide for
Growing, Protecting, and Using Your Money*

Patrick Blair

Faith and Finances
A 21st Century Biblical Guide for Growing, Protecting and Using Your Money
© 2019 by Patrick Blair

All rights reserved. No part of this book may be duplicated, copied, translated, reproduced or stored mechanically or electronically without specific, written permission of the author and publisher.

ISBN: 978-1-948450-44-7. Printed in the United States. Illumination Publishers cares deeply about the environment and uses recycled paper whenever possible.

All Scripture quotations, unless indicated, are taken from the *Holy Bible, New International Version,* (NIV), Copyright © 2011, 2015 by Biblica, Inc. Used by permission. All rights reserved worldwide.

The Holy Bible, New King James Version. Copyright © 1982 by Thomas Nelson, Inc. All rights reserved.

Holy Bible, New Living Translation copyright © 1996, 2004, 2007 by Tyndale House Foundation. Used by permission of Tyndale House Publishers Inc.

Cover design by Roy Appalsamy of Toronto, Canada. Interior book design by Toney Mulhollan.

About the author: After serving in church leadership for many years, Patrick Blair began his career as a civil litigation attorney in the Los Angeles area. After experiencing personal hardship with debt and professionally working with debtors, he developed a keen interest in how people manage their money, including related social and economic trends.

Patrick holds a Juris Doctorate from the University of Hawaii, where he also obtained undergraduate degrees in Psychology and Speech. Patrick is a practicing attorney, who lives with his wife and two children in Oak Ridge, NC.

www.ipibooks.com
6010 Pinecreek Ridge Court
Spring, Texas 77379-2513

CONTENTS

Foreword 6
Preface 8

Section I: The Basics
Chapter 1: Honor God with Your Wealth 16
Chapter 2: Spend Less Than You Make 34
Chapter 3: Aggressively Pay Off Debt 38
Chapter 4: Save 46

Section II: Biblical Perspectives on Wealth
Chapter 5: From Slave to Slave Master 54
Chapter 6: Mastering Mammon 58
Chapter 7: Custodians of Wealth 63
Chapter 8: The Deceptions of Wealth 68
Chapter 9: Riches and Righteousness 77
Chapter 10: Worry and Money 91

Section III: Financial Investments
Chapter 11: Diversification & Other Biblical Financial Advice .. 102
Chapter 12: Wall Street Investments 117
Chapter 13: Other Investments 124
Chapter 14: Alternative Investments 138

Section IV: Spiritual Investments
Chapter 15: Motivations for Charitable Giving 153
Chapter 16: Giving More 160
Chapter 17: Giving to the Poor 168
Chapter 18: Evangelism and Missions 176
Final Thoughts 184

Topical Index 185
Acknowledgements 191
Endnotes 192

PLEASE READ THESE TERMS OF USE:

This book is not intended to represent a definitive source of information on the subjects of personal finance, financial biblical theology, investments, or charitable giving, but is rather intended to simplify, elucidate, complement, and supplement other available sources.

Despite the best efforts and intentions of the author and publisher, this book may contain mistakes, and the reader should use the book as a general guide and not as the ultimate source of advice or information about the subject of this book.

The author and publisher of this book are not financial experts. If the reader desires personal and professional financial advice, he or she should seek the services of a competent financial expert.

Every individual is responsible for adapting the contents of this book to their specific needs and situations.

This book is sold without warranties of any kind, express or implied, and the publisher and author disclaim any liability, loss, or damage caused by the contents of this book. Any loss or damage incurred is the sole responsibility of the reader and is the result of the reader's own decisions.

If you do not wish to be bound by the foregoing cautions and conditions, you may return the book to the publisher for a full refund.

Legal Disclaimer: I (the author) am a lawyer, but not your lawyer. This book is for educational purposes only. Nothing in this book is meant to be legal, tax, or investment advice. If you have any legal or tax questions, please consult a qualified attorney or C.P.A. in your jurisdiction. You are solely responsible for all of your investment decisions.

—To my dear family:

Audrey, Kennedy, and Kyle

Foreword

I've been giving financial advice for over thirty-eight years as a tax lawyer and CPA in private practice in Athens, Georgia. I've seen the financial ups and downs of thousands of clients and see how the Bible's wisdom rings true in every situation. Although I have done well in my business and finances, I've experienced how important it is to hold fast to the Scriptures in every way.

As a son of a Cuban immigrants, I grew up humbly and was always taught to save money and avoid debt. Even though my mother had only a sixth-grade education and made close to minimum wage, she managed to raise two children and amass a significant amount of wealth over her lifetime. Beginning in 1995, I gave my first of many financial workshops in various churches throughout the country which featured biblical wealth principles, lessons I learned from my mother, and interesting stories about my clients (anonymously, of course).

Again and again, I've seen debt destroy, disrupt, and degrade people's lives. I've also seen how wealth can be a true blessing, enriching people's lives and giving them the freedom to do mini-mission trips or take several months off to go help brothers and sisters throughout the world. I firmly believe that the ability to handle the money that comes into our lives is a critically important tool for our lives and faith. Never before has there been so much complexity, confusion and temptation when it comes to money as there is today.

So many Christians and non-Christians alike are enslaved to debt and ignorant of the dynamics that cause their suffering. Despite having great hearts, many Christians make poor decisions that hold back and even damage their faith. Likewise, some Christians' faith is held back by their great wealth. In my talks, I compare wealth to a multi-headed snake. It's a powerful thing that can help you accomplish a lot but can also bite you and shipwreck your faith.

I have spoken to many audiences over the years since that first talk in 1995. They always seemed to love hearing about my mother and how well she managed money despite having little education and a low earning ability. It's proof that anyone can do well financially if certain basic principles are followed. My audiences also loved hearing rarely taught Scriptures about handling money and how to do well spiritually in the process.

After one such seminar, I was approached by the author of this book, and asked, "Why haven't you written a book?" A few moments later, Patrick put a copy of his manuscript in my hand. I told him I would read it on the flight back home later that evening. I found it so good that I couldn't put it down! The book encompassed so much of what I had been presenting in my seminars and so much more.

After getting to know more about Patrick, I realized that his background as an attorney and his long history of service to the church made him the perfect person to write this modern, up-to-date guide about Christian finances. Not everyone can have a mother like mine or a financial practice from which to glean wisdom, but with this book and an open heart, Christians can become wise, financially successful and generous. The well-rounded, analytical style of the book will appeal to both your logic and your faith.

I've always had a passion to help people both spiritually and financially. I'm excited that Patrick shares that passion and has written this comprehensive book covering the subject biblically and practically. Whenever I give a seminar or talk to people about this subject, I'll highly recommend that my listeners read this book!

—Greg Garcia, C.P.A., J.D.
Athens, GA

Preface

As a young Christian, I thought that giving attention to money was beneath me. I was following the mighty Jesus Christ and had moved beyond such things! I spent and gave freely, which for a time was mentally liberating. At some point I realized I was being lazy and shortsighted, deferring my labor into the future.

I honestly wish that as Christians we could ignore financial matters and only focus on other seemingly more spiritual matters. It would make our lives much simpler, but that just isn't how God designed our reality. I slowly learned that my overly-simplistic view of handling money was hurting my long-term finances and holding me back from spiritual growth.

Instead of ethereal creatures, God made human beings into flesh and bone. He created us from the dust of the earth—to be both physical and spiritual beings. From the very beginning, God designed us to work and to survive in this material world. We are both humbled and driven by our physical and emotional needs.

Even in this modern age, we suffer from the curse of Adam and are forced to work hard to make a living. In one way or another, we manage money day in and day out. We cannot escape its grasp. I'll even go so far as to say that wealth and the handling of wealth are the means by which God shapes our earthly destinies.

As you will see in the chapters to come, God is very concerned with how we handle wealth. He gives tremendous attention to the subject in his word. Both the Old and New Testaments are filled with wisdom, warnings, examples and philosophies regarding the handling of wealth.

ABOUT THE AUTHOR

When I was ten, I got my first savings account, which included a little account booklet that was updated whenever I visited the bank. At the time, I received about 5% interest and was very excited whenever I saw the ledger entries, because my money was earning money! It was so simple, and I thought I had money all figured out. Little did I know how my upbringing would indelibly etch complex fears, aspirations and perspectives about money into my psyche.

I grew up middle class on the Big Island of Hawaii, with parents who struggled with and worried a lot about money. My mother owned a series of retail gift and jewelry stores. When sales were down, she would work long hours to cut down on labor costs. She would close stores that weren't doing well and open new ones with different product lines to fit changing trends. We even moved to the west side of the Island when tourism shifted away from east side. I lived in eight different places by the time I finished high school.

My father worked various jobs and struggled to put together a stable career. During and between jobs, he would work with my mother. He was a talented person but was unable to find a solid career until he hit his 50s, which is very unusual. My father had ongoing health problems and passed away in 2004. After a lifetime of hard work, he was very concerned that his health problems might bankrupt our family. Thankfully, they didn't.

Until the last few years of my father's life, my parents didn't have savings or investments to speak of. In part, they were unable to accumulate wealth because they had terrible timing when it came to buying and selling the family homes we lived in. The few investments they made were duds.

My family didn't have much disposable income, but when it came to my advancement, my parents spared no expense. My mother would not so subtly express to me her expectations that I would excel academically and become successful. I resented and rebelled against the pressure, but I ultimately took on the mindset she trained me to have. Consciously and unconsciously, my parents passed on their fears, failures, and aspirations to me.

What experience did you have with wealth (or lack of wealth) growing up? What fears, failures, and aspirations has your family passed on to you? I believe it's worth reflecting on these things, because they can give you valuable insight into your feelings and motivations.

> **What experience did you have with wealth (or lack of wealth) growing up? What fears, failures, and aspirations has your family passed on to you?**

My parents wanted me to be successful and pushed me academically. It's amazing how an idea implanted within you grows, possibly even beyond its intended goal. For better or worse, I carry a never-ending sense that I have to achieve and that nothing is ever good enough.

I never made it my goal to be rich, but like every other kid, I wanted to buy things and do things. I engaged in all sorts of entrepreneurial activities to make sure I had the means to buy what I wanted. I mowed lawns, picked fruit, sold things and eventually worked formal jobs. I learned, as everyone does, that if I wanted things in life, I had to have money to pay for those things.

In college, I pursued my interest in human behavior by studying psychology, but when I neared completion of my degree, I realized that it wasn't going to lead me to gainful employment. Like many aimless college graduates, I ended up going to law school, where I learned about the mechanics of society.

Throughout my undergraduate and law school years, I held firm to my faith and served in church leadership. Off and on, I worked as a paid minister in both Hawaii and Los Angeles. Even when I wasn't being paid, I participated in church leadership at whatever level I could. Although I liked many aspects of working as a paid minister, I didn't feel it was the best fit for me.

As I'll talk about later in the book, starting in 1999 I came on hard times financially and in my career. During the 2008 foreclosure crisis, I practiced law as a litigator defending mortgage servicers from lending liability claims. From the confluence of my background and early career, I started to develop a keen interest in how people manage their money, including related social and economic trends.

I'm not a financial planner, economist or personal finance guru. I'm not a Bible scholar or career preacher. I'm just a "Joe Christian" who has struggled to do what is right before God during the ups and downs of my life. I don't need to be an expert to know that what really matters is that, in the end, God says to me:

> *"His Master replied, 'Well done, good and faithful servant! You have been faithful with a few things; I will put you in charge of many things. Come and share your master's happiness!' (Matthew 25:21)*

In particular, I've grappled with my ambitions and my wealth and how that fits into my Christian life. I've had some victories, but I write as one who is constantly humbled by my failures as well. Truly, God's *"power is made perfect in weakness"* (2 Corinthians 12:9).

WHAT THIS BOOK IS ABOUT

I've studied, observed, and searched for answers and in this book, I share those with you. I sincerely hope you can benefit from my perspective and the Scriptures within. I initially set out to write a book just about Christian financial investing, but as I wrote, I realized that the topic didn't carry much power because it was being told in a vacuum. I felt it was critical to present the whole picture. My goal is to deliver a sense of wholeness to a topic that on the surface appears to be divided into discrete parts.

This book is meant to be a comprehensive guide for Christians in handling their wealth. Most Christian books about money cover one or two of the following areas: 1) personal finance basics, 2) biblical wealth principles, 3) biblical investing principles, and 4) Christian giving. This book covers all four! Keep in mind that first and foremost, this is a spiritual book meant to help keep you near to God.

What do we do with the wealth that God gives us? Do we spend it on ourselves, make financial investments, or generously give it away? What exactly does God want us to do with our wealth? Rather than using the Bible to back up my opinions or agenda, I've taken great care to survey the entire Bible in context to get a well-rounded picture.[1] Let's explore that together in the chapters ahead.

Of course, no person can tell you specifically what you should do with your wealth, nor should they. That's your decision and your decision alone. Only you know what really goes on in that area of your life. My goal is to sensitize you to what the Scriptures say on the subject in order to help you make godly decisions.

I've lived in Hawaii, California, and in North Carolina, so the book is U.S.-centric, but I believe that you can apply the principles and ideas anywhere you live in the world. You may need to adjust what is being said to your context. I quote a lot of Scriptures and have them separated and indented for ease of reading. Sometimes, I discuss an idea and support it with a Scripture; at other times, I start with the Scripture and then discuss it. I use the differing patterns to enhance reading flow.

> The book is U.S.-centric, but I believe that you can apply the principles and ideas anywhere you live in the world. You may need to adjust what is being said to your context.

If you have a particular need or interest, I hope this book can guide you in your search for answers. The book is divided into four distinct sections and organized by specific topics that you can skip to if you like. The four sections are meant to foster: 1) financial discipline, 2) a healthy perspective about money, 3) wealth growth, and

4) godly generosity. However, I highly recommend that you read the book from beginning to end to get the full picture.

Rather than merely being informed, my hope is that this book and the Scriptures within will help you be transformed. What vision do you have for your life? Does it involve serving God, making a positive impact on the world, and personally prospering? Whatever your visions, the way you handle wealth will either be a stumbling block or a catalyst.

As humans, we tend to think in narratives like stories, books, and movies. Even the way we view our own life is a narrative. What's going on in that story and where will it go? So often, the story we tell ourselves about ourselves eventually shapes our lives. What is the story in which you will live your life?

I encourage you to take a few minutes to jot down your major life goals, both secular and spiritual. Try not to self-censor what you write (you can always re-evaluate your goals). Write down what you really desire in your heart.

Section I:
THE BASICS

First Things First

It should go without saying: before you can invest, you need to have wealth. But our debt-dependent, credit-infested world has blurred what should be obvious. Some of us have money in investment accounts, but we also carry consumer debt. If that's the case, odds are you are paying more in interest than you are gaining in investments.

Desire without knowledge is not good—
how much more will hasty feet miss the way!
(Proverbs 19:2)

It's easy to get ahead of ourselves financially. We want to play the investment game or be generous to others without really having wealth, but it's not a good plan. Put your oxygen mask on first, before helping those seated next to you.

In theory you can have consumer debt and still invest, but you've got three big strikes against you. First, mathematically speaking, you're fighting an uphill battle. When you invest, there's no guarantee you're going to make money. But when you accrue interest on debt, you are guaranteed a loss.

Second, you won't have allowed yourself to fully develop the discipline of spending less than you make. The process of paying down debt shapes your habits. Those habits pay life-long dividends in the form of disciplined spending.

Third, you won't have allowed yourself to develop the winning psychology you need to succeed at investing. Paying off consumer debt is a huge accomplishment for most people. It is a milestone that gives you confidence.

If you're struggling with consumer debt, take heart! God is using this time to shape you into his image. You are developing integrity, honesty, patience, and perseverance. The month by month grind of paying down debt is exactly what the doctor ordered. To build wealth, you must master the basics.

THE BASICS

There is a veritable cornucopia of material about personal finance, which is one of the reasons I chose not to cover it extensively.

First Things First

I started out watching The Suze Orman Show (2002-2015), which I found both educational and entertaining. Sometimes, you need some sugar to make the medicine go down!

I also really enjoyed a book my dad introduced me to: *The Richest Man in Babylon*, by George S. Clason.[2] The book is actually a collection of pamphlets given out by banks and insurance companies in the 1920s. It is written in a parable style and set in ancient Babylon, which gives it the mystique of ancient wisdom.

At the time of this writing, Christian financial education is dominated by Dave Ramsey.

> **WARNING:** Even if you are currently wealthy, you need to continue to follow the basics.

Whether coming from a Christian or secular point of view, personal finance practicals are very similar. You could even say that personal finance wisdom is universal, with a few exceptions. Whatever keeps you motivated to follow the basics: do it!

Warning: Even if you are currently wealthy, you need to continue to follow the basics. We've all heard of many professional athletes, celebrities and lottery winners who are now flat broke. They all have one thing in common: they didn't follow financial basics.

There are many ways to peel the onion, so to speak. I encourage you to find what works for you, whether it is my system or someone else's. I call my system the Four Rules of Spiritual Finances:

1. **Honor God with your wealth**
2. **Spend less than you make**
3. **Aggressively pay off bad debt**
4. **Save**

Understanding these rules is easy but following them is not.

Chapter 1
Honor God with Your Wealth

Honor the LORD with your wealth,
with the firstfruits of all your crops;
then your barns will be filled to overflowing,
and your vats will brim over with new wine.
(Proverbs 3:9-10)

There's no question that God deserves honor, because he created us, our wealth, our world and our whole universe. You may think that the Perfect Being should not need honor, but like any parent he does. Because he created us and loves us unconditionally, it's fitting that we honor our Heavenly Father.

We may honor God through prayer and song, by avoiding sin, and teaching others about his son Jesus. But do we really honor him, if we don't also honor him with our wealth? I hope your wealth is not in a cordoned off area of your heart, reserved only for yourself.

There are many ways to honor God with your wealth, which are discussed throughout this book. This chapter is focused on giving to your local congregation. By extension, this chapter is also about establishing a baseline standard of giving.

OFFERINGS ARE PART OF OUR RELATIONSHIP WITH GOD

Now Abel kept flocks, and Cain worked the soil. In the course of time Cain brought some of the fruits of the soil as an offering to the LORD. And Abel also brought an offering—fat portions from some of the firstborn of his flock. The Lord looked with favor on Abel and his offering, but on Cain and his offering he did not look with favor. So Cain was very angry, and his face was downcast.

Then the LORD said to Cain, "Why are you angry? Why is your face downcast? If you do what is right, will you not be accepted? But if you do not do what is right, sin is crouching at your door; it desires to have you, but you must rule over it." (Genesis 4:2b-8)

From the very beginning, man sought to honor God with offerings. When we give to our church, it's really an offering to God. The concept of an offering might seem primitive, but our modern hearts still yearn to please God and we deeply desire his approval.

Cain, the farmer, brought *"some of the fruits of the soil as an offering to the LORD,"* for which God was not pleased. Different translations say that God did not accept, did not respect, or did not have regard for Cain's offering. The Bible then contrasts Cain's offering with his brother Abel's offering.

Abel, the shepherd, brought *"fat portions from some of the firstborn of his flock."* God favored Abel's offering, because it was *"of the firstborn"* of his flock. Also, he offered "fat portions," which were the best part. Cain did not give his firstfruits or the best of his harvest.

We know the rest of the tragic story. It's hard to tell exactly what Cain was thinking. Perhaps his offering was blatantly hypocritical, and he just offered a few damaged and diseased fruits, which would have been an insult to God. Or maybe Cain's offering was sincere, but he simply held back his whole heart. Either way, Cain became very bitter with God.

WORK YOUR ISSUES OUT WITH GOD

The story of Cain and Abel carries a poignant message for us all. When we give our best to God, we feel approved of by God. When we don't and are challenged on it, we're tempted to be resentful. Of course, we all fail in many ways and feel disapproved of at times. That's why it's so important to be in touch with our anger and to work things out with God before our hearts become bitter.

> **How we give financially and in other areas reflects our relationship with God.**

You may be wondering what all of this has to do with financial giving. Well, how we feel about God will ultimately shape our financial giving. How we give financially and in other areas reflects our relationship with God. It's easy to become resentful toward God when we don't feel things are going our way.

Some of us don't want to acknowledge our anger, because we

think it's taboo to be angry with or question God. That couldn't be further from the truth. Major characters in the Old Testament, like Moses, Job, David, Jeremiah, and Jonah, all take issue with God at some point and come out better for it. This pattern is found repeatedly in the Bible. That's why it's so important to work things out with God in prayer, especially when you feel angry and disapproved of.

> *By faith Abel brought God a better offering than Cain did. By faith he was commended as righteous, when God spoke well of his offerings. And by faith Abel still speaks, even though he is dead.* (Hebrews 11:4)

Cain's "actions were evil and his brother's were righteous" (1 John 3:12). Abel's offering was given in faith and God considered him righteous. Is our offering to God righteous or half-hearted? Maybe even considering this question makes your heart feel like Cain's did, when he felt resentful. I know it can sometimes feel that way for me. Rather than simply telling ourselves what we give is enough, we need to search the Scriptures for guidance, so that we can truly be approved of by God.

WE HAVE A RESPONSIBILITY TO SUPPORT THE CHURCH

> *Don't you know that those who serve in the temple get their food from the temple, and that those who serve at the altar share in what is offered on the altar? In the same way, the Lord has commanded that those who preach the gospel should receive their living from the gospel.*
> (1 Corinthians 9:13-14)

Temple and altar servants took from the offerings to support themselves. Likewise, we have a direct New Covenant command to support our preachers through offerings. Although we are all called to proclaim the good news, some of us need to make it our careers to do so, just as some of the Levites did for Israel.

Just as the tribes of Israel were responsible for supporting the Levitical priesthood, Christians are responsible for supporting the church. Similarly, preachers and other paid servants of the church have a special responsibility to the flock under their care. Of course, we all have many "one another" spiritual responsibilities, but paid leaders should be especially conscientious and trustworthy.

One Christian I spoke with on this subject said that he didn't feel like he was sacrificing when he gave his weekly offering to the church. He felt that he was merely doing his part. Although on the surface his view might appear secular, I believe it has strong support in the Scriptures. When the Israelites failed to properly support their priesthood, it started a viscous cycle of spiritual decay. We know the same thing can happen in our local congregations.

> *"We also assume responsibility for bringing to the house of the LORD each year the firstfruits of our crops and of every fruit tree.*
> *"As it is also written in the Law, we will bring the firstborn of our sons and of our cattle, of our herds and of our flocks to the house of our God, to the priests ministering there. .... We will not neglect the house of our God."*
> (Nehemiah 10:35-36, 39b)

It took heart and offerings to build the Kingdom in Nehemiah's time. It still does today! A lack of giving keeps a lid on the gospel. It keeps church-supported ministers from being hired. It keeps the poor from being served. It suppresses the glory of God. Will you assume responsibility for your giving?

FOLLOWING CHRIST'S EXAMPLE

> *For you know the grace of our Lord Jesus Christ, that though he was rich, yet for your sake he became poor, so that you through his poverty might become rich.*
> (2 Corinthians 8:9)

Think about it: Jesus willingly left the magnificence of heaven for our sakes. He came so that we could have the spiritual wealth of the forgiveness of our sins, which he considered more precious than his time behind the pearly gates. Of course, his time away from heaven was temporary, just as is our time here on earth.

As a general proposition, I could say that we should all be 100% righteous and sacrificial in everything since Christ was that way. I'm not a big fan of thinking like that because perfection is impossible, too overwhelming and not specific enough to motivate us. The point

I am making is very specific: Jesus temporarily gave up his riches for our souls, so we can do the same for ourselves and others. If a church is generous and its leadership is trustworthy, it's well-positioned to grow and thrive.

HOW MUCH SHOULD WE GIVE?

We all know we should give to our church, but the amount is the really the big question, isn't it? The answer is not necessarily 10% (a tithe), which I will explain later. The answer is not just enough to meet some minimum expectation. The answer also not to give in a way that puts us or keeps us in debt.

So, what is the answer? The best simple answer is that we should give whatever we've "decided in our hearts to give, not reluctantly or under compulsion." (2 Corinthians 9:7). I say "simple" answer, but it's really not that simple.

There are many things to consider when deciding what to give, which we will explore throughout this book. Thanks for opening your mind and heart to exploring this subject with me. I will attempt to take great care in being biblically accurate and sensitive to real-life issues. I will also take great care in guiding you toward a good, long-term financial situation, because I believe that is just as biblical as sacrifice.

We need to first set a baseline expectation for ourselves. We may set that expectation and not meet it. We may exceed it. As our income and life situation changes, we can re-evaluate and reset our baseline giving amount.

I believe this dynamic to be a good thing. Without it, we would be left with our mood swings when it comes to giving. If you give on a weekly or even a monthly basis, it would be a strange and burdensome task to have to decide before each offering what you feel like giving. When we have a baseline, it gives us a benchmark in which to objectively measure how much we are really sacrificing. It also provides an automatic check to guard us against materialism and overspending.

WHY DID GOD NOT MAKE IT CLEAR HOW MUCH WE SHOULD GIVE?

Rather than robotically applying a rule, I believe that God wants us to examine our heart for giving, just as we should regularly examine our heart for everything else that is for God (1 Corinthians 11:28; 2 Corinthians 13:5). God also wants our giving to be from the heart, which isn't necessarily the same thing as giving out of emotion.

> So I thought it necessary to urge the brothers to visit you in advance and finish the arrangements for the generous gift you had promised. Then it will be ready as a generous gift, not as one grudgingly given.
> Remember this: Whoever sows sparingly will also reap sparingly, and whoever sows generously will also reap generously. Each of you should give what you have decided in your heart to give, not reluctantly or under compulsion, for God loves a cheerful giver. (2 Corinthians 9:5-7)

It is important to be clear: this passage doesn't deal with regular giving to the church. Paul was conducting a specific fundraiser to assist the Judean churches that were undergoing a great famine. I believe, however, the principles behind Paul's directive applies to all giving. God is more concerned with our attitude when we give, than how much we give. He wants us to give with joy! That's why he wants us to choose the amount.

If giving a specific amount or percentage were commanded, it would become compulsory. If it were compulsory, it would be virtually impossible for it to be given from the heart. It would be more like taxes. We may be patriotic, but do we give our taxes from the heart? No, but we give gifts from our heart.

So, God wants us to give from the heart, which is not at all the same thing as having a low standard. We shouldn't interpret this passage to mean we should give so little that we couldn't possibly be reluctant. Rather, we should push and stretch our faith, because we reap spiritually what we sow materially. When we generously give in faith, God is very pleased!

WHAT ABOUT USING THE TITHE AS A MODEL FOR GIVING?

Although I could give blunt conclusions on this subject, I believe this culturally complex and sensitive topic deserves a nuanced explanation. In the development of this book, no topic has proven to be more controversial or complex than the tithe. Admittedly, I originally wrote this entire chapter with the tithe as its central theme, because I believed it provided a solid biblical standard for baseline giving. After input from bible scholars and further research, I rewrote this entire chapter in a manner that I believe more properly reflects biblical offerings.

For some individuals, the tithe can be a good baseline standard for giving. For many, it provides a compelling conceptual and practical foundation for which to view their offerings to God. Over the years, it has been very helpful to me. It's an easy standard to understand, internalize, and teach. As convenient as the rule is, it should never replace the New Testament teachings about generous offerings given in faith.

> **Instead of teaching the deeper reasons why Christians should generously give to the church, it's much easier to point to the tithe.**

Instead of teaching the deeper reasons why Christians should generously give to the church, it's much easier to point to the tithe. Rather than examining our hearts and faith for giving, it's much easier to apply the simple rule of 10%. Some Christians might be unfamiliar with the underlying concept, because it's hardly mentioned in the New Testament. Neither Jesus nor his apostles taught that we should tithe to the church. Let me explain.

WHAT IS A TITHE?

Let's unpack this complex issue piece by piece. A tithe literally means a tenth. The tithe was a tax in which the Israelites gave a tenth of their herds and agricultural products, which was to be given to the Levites (the Israelite priesthood) and to the poor (Deuteronomy 14:27-29). The Old Testament law commanded a tithe:

> *A tithe of everything from the land, whether grain from the soil or fruit from the trees, belongs to the Lord; it is holy to the LORD.* (Leviticus 27:30)

> *Every tithe of the herd and flock—every tenth animal that passes under the shepherd's rod—will be holy to the Lord. No one may pick out the good from the bad or make any substitution.* (Leviticus 27:32-33a)

Most of the wealth generated two thousand years ago came from raising crops and animals. So, the tithe tax was widespread and affected the majority of the population on some level. It was significant enough to support an entire tribe of Israel and to assist the poor.

You may be wondering about the distinction between the "firstfruits" and the tithe. The two can sometimes be referred to as the same thing, but frankly their exact connection is unclear. Perhaps because Israel was an evolving society and the first-fruits/tithes' practical function changed over time, that gave rise to their shifting roles.[3] Technically, they are different concepts, however, some Scriptures treat them as if they are interchangeable (Deuteronomy 26:1-15).

It is difficult to analogize the tithe to modern day offerings for a host of reasons. The tithe was a tax and not an offering. The Israelites also had many offerings, some required and some voluntary. Just as we do, the Israelites had various taxes imposed by differing levels of government. The Israelite government was, at least on some level, a theocracy, whereas most governments today are purely secular. So, comparisons between today and ancient Israel are not apples-to-apples comparisons on many levels.

AREN'T WE FREE FROM OLD TESTAMENT LAW ANYWAY?

Yes, as Christians we are not bound by Mosaic Law. The New Covenant is nearly ritual free, except for the Lord's Supper. Just because we are now without the Mosaic Law, does not mean the past laws did not have great wisdom and spiritual significance.

We're not obligated to conduct animal sacrifices or cleansing rituals, but it is important to recognize there are consequences for our sins. We do not need to observe the sabbath, but regularly resting from work is a wise practice. Christmas, Easter, and other observances are cultural traditions, but can be helpful to our spirit if observed correctly.

The tithe also falls by the wayside along with all the other Mosaic Laws, but as with all the other laws, there is a beneficial idea behind the Old Testament practice. The tithe showed us to honor God with a portion of what he allowed us to have. Something also to consider is that the giving of a tenth and Firstfruits (Genesis 4:2b-8) predates the Mosaic Law.

> *Then Melchizedek king of Salem brought out bread and wine. He was [the] priest of God Most High, and he blessed Abram, saying,*
> *"Blessed be Abram by God Most High,*
> *Creator of heaven and earth.*
> *And praise be to God Most High,*
> *who delivered your enemies into your hand."*

> *Then Abram gave him a tenth of everything.*
> (Genesis 14:18-20)

The tenth Abram gave to Melchizedek was a sign of respect and honor. It was an acknowledgement that his victory and the spoils of war came from God. Jesus himself was a priest in the order of Melchizedek (Hebrews 5:6, Psalm 110:1-4). Abram's grandson, Jacob, also pledged to give God a tenth (Genesis 28:20-22). Although the tithe is not now required, we can still learn a lot from it.

WHAT DOES THE NEW TESTAMENT SAY ABOUT THE TITHE?

The tithe is not directly addressed in the New Testament. However, there are passages that use it to illustrate other spiritual concepts.

> *This Melchizedek was king of Salem and priest of God Most High. He met Abraham returning from the defeat of the kings and blessed him, and Abraham gave him a tenth of everything. First, the name Melchizedek means "king of righteousness"; then also, "king of Salem" means "king of peace." Without father or mother, without genealogy, without beginning of days or end of life, resembling the Son of God, he remains a priest forever.* (Hebrews 7:1-3)

This is a fascinating passage about the identity of Melchizedek. His holiness and otherworldly qualities made him superior to Levi and his descendants. The passage then makes the connection to Jesus' priesthood and its supremacy over the Levitical priesthood.

> *Just think how great he was: Even the patriarch Abraham gave him a tenth of the plunder! Now the law requires the descendants of Levi who become priests to collect a tenth from the people—that is, from their fellow Israelites—even though they also are descended from Abraham. This man, however, did not trace his descent from Levi, yet he collected a tenth from Abraham and blessed him who had the promises. And without doubt the lesser is blessed by the greater. In the one case, the tenth is collected by people who die; but in the other case, by him who is declared to be living. One might even say that Levi, who collects the tenth, paid*

> *the tenth through Abraham, because when Melchizedek met Abraham, Levi was still in the body of his ancestor.*
> (Hebrews 7:4-10)

As support for Jesus' supremacy, the Hebrew writer uses the fact that Abraham gave Melchizedek a tenth (Genesis 14:20). One could argue that if Levi was due a tenth, then so should Jesus (being a priest in the order of Melchizedek). However, that would be a stretch since the point of the passage is clearly not tithe giving.

The New Testament uses the tithe to illustrate another point. Jesus said:

> *"Woe to you, teachers of the law and Pharisees, you hypocrites! You give a tenth of your spices—mint, dill and cumin. But you have neglected the more important matters of the law—justice, mercy and faithfulness. You should have practiced the latter, without neglecting the former."* (Matthew 23:23)

Jesus accused the Pharisees of pretending to be obedient to God, because they neglected justice, mercy and faithfulness—core qualities of God. He contrasts this with their dutiful adherence to the tithe. We can be the same way! We can take great care to follow detailed church etiquette. We can make regular offerings but miss the big picture.

On a technical note, Jesus did say they should continue their tithing. He said: *"You should have practiced [justice, mercy and faithfulness], without neglecting [the tithe]."* On an equally technical note, the Pharisees were obligated under Moses' law to give a tithe of their produce, even herbs. So, Jesus was merely confirming their Mosaic obligation, which has no bearing on Christians. Even modern-day Jews do not tithe, because there is no Temple or Levitical priesthood.

WHAT ABOUT THE SCRIPTURE IN MALACHI 3 ABOUT ROBBING GOD?

> *"Will a mere mortal rob God? Yet you rob me.*
> *"But you ask, 'How are we robbing you?'*
> *"In tithes and offerings. You are under a curse—your whole nation—because you are robbing me. Bring the whole tithe into the storehouse, that there may be food in my house.*

Test me in this," says the LORD Almighty, "and see if I will not throw open the floodgates of heaven and pour out so much blessing that there will not be room enough to store it. I will prevent pests from devouring your crops, and the vines in your fields will not drop their fruit before it is ripe," says the LORD Almighty. "Then all the nations will call you blessed, for yours will be a delightful land," says the LORD Almighty. (Malachi 3:8-12)

Although Christians are not the nation of Israel and no longer bound to the tithe tax, there is much to be learned from this passage. God said he was being robbed, because the tithes and offerings were his! It was the Israelites duty to give their tithes and offerings to support their temple and temple servants. Isn't the situation for Christians very similar today?

I'm not going to go so far as to say that everything in this passage applies in the same ways to Christians, but I think the spirit of the passage applies. In my opinion, the main thing for a Christian to understand here is that when the church as a whole is generous, God will bless it tremendously. God often takes a small effort (mustard seed) from his followers and does amazing things with it. God just wants our hearts and faith, and he does the heavy lifting.

> **You see, giving is really about honoring God for who he is: master of all. When you boil it down, offerings are really an issue of faith.**

Another principle you might glean from this passage is that giving to God is more about faith than sacrifice. Think about where your wealth comes from and who keeps you away from financial disaster. Who has the power to give you even more? You see, giving is really about honoring God for who he is: master of all. When you boil it down, offerings are really an issue of faith.

AS CHRISTIANS, SHOULDN'T WE GIVE MORE THAN A TENTH?

We shouldn't just be shooting for the minimum, right? That's a great sentiment, but if you've been carefully reading thus far, you realize that we are not required to give a tenth in the first place. Even though it's based on a false assumption, I thought it would be a good idea to briefly entertain this question.

If the tithe as a number is irrelevant, then in theory, our offerings have no minimum. On the same token, our offerings also have no maximum. There's no specific percentage benchmark to measure from. So, the answer to whether we should give more than a tenth is: not necessarily. God wants you to choose what you want to give without some pre-determined benchmark, but don't let that fact be a license for greed. Let the choice be a chance to examine your faith and generously give from your heart.

WHAT KEEPS US FROM GENEROUS OFFERINGS?

Let me first say that generosity is a very subjective concept and that what is generous varies from person to person, situation to situation, country to country, region to region, etc. But let's discuss the concept in general terms. A recent study showed that U.S. church members, on average, give 2.3% of their income to their local congregation.[4] Sadly, the study highlights the slow and steady decrease in church giving over the decades.

I'm going to go out on a limb and say that for the great majority of church goers in the U.S., 2.3% giving is not generous. If you think your congregation gives a lot more than 2.3%, think again. Remember, we're talking about an average. I strongly suspect the average mostly consists of a small percentage of people giving generously, and the rest giving a token amount. Perhaps it's the 80/20 principle in action?

What that means for many is that they give only a pittance to their church, maybe 1% or less. So, a person or family who makes $50,000 per year giving 1%, would put about $10 in the plate each week. That same person or family giving 2.3% would put in about $22. Could anyone in good conscience believe that such giving is honoring God?

When a person or family gives at this level or doesn't give at all, I am concerned for their spiritual well-being. Keep in mind that I don't work for a church or have a paid minister's mindset. I'm not just making a plug for church revenue. Having worked in small group leadership for decades, I've worked with many people and sincerely care about their spiritual and emotional condition. This Scripture is very instructive in this situation:

> *And we urge you, brothers and sisters, warn those who are idle and disruptive, encourage the disheartened, help the weak, be patient with everyone.* (1 Thessalonians 5:14)

I've observed that there are five basic reasons why Christians don't generously give in faith.

1. **They Have Not Been Taught.** They simply need to be taught and will quickly start giving in faith. You'd be surprised how often this is the case.
2. **They Misunderstand the Biblical Principles.** They need to have an honest bible study on the subject. Maybe reading a book like this one can help.
3. **They Lack the Character Not to Overspend.** In this case, they are most likely in debt and need help with their personal finances. We are all in this category to some degree!
4. **They Have No Income.** They have little or nothing to give because they are out of work or their business is going badly. This brings up a whole host of other issues outside the scope of this book. In general, they need help, encouragement, and prayer. I've personally been there many times and it can really take a toll your faith. Be loving to people in this situation!
5. **They Have an Emergency.** They have little or nothing to give because they have an emergency or important ongoing family need (typically medical or elderly support issues). This really shouldn't be on this list, because people in this situation might be generously giving in faith (just not to their church). I just wanted to make sure we all consider this.
6. **Compromise is Eroding Their Faith.** They may be involved in serious sin, bitter with God, bitter with others, and/or disgruntled with church. Giving generously is often the first thing to go in these situations. Anyone in this situation needs help right away!

Take a moment to evaluate your own faith and situation. What can you do to help yourself and others in these areas?

NEW TESTAMENT WISDOM ON HOW WE SHOULD GIVE

We've discussed how offerings are a part of our relationship with God, why we should give, and how much we should give. But what else can we learn from the Scriptures about how to give offerings?

REGULAR OFFERINGS

Now about the collection for the Lord's people: Do what I told the Galatian churches to do. On the first day of every week, each one of you should set aside a sum of money in keeping with your income, saving it up, so that when I come no collections will have to be made. (1 Corinthians 16:1-2)

Paul guided the Galatian and Corinthian churches to set aside an offering for supporting the Judean churches each Sunday. Why give once each week? I believe it's just common sense. If you give regularly, it helps you budget and keeps you from spending your offering.

Although giving once a week isn't a biblical command, it's a good practice. For some, giving once a month makes sense if you get paid monthly. Some like to give in larger chunks less often for similar reasons. Regular giving is good because it's one of many regular things you can do to keep in touch with God.

PROPORTIONAL OFFERINGS

We've already talked about setting a baseline percentage of your income for your offering, but what about having a baseline that is not based on a percentage of your income? Could someone come up with some other kind of system based on other metrics? Perhaps you could have an emotional standard like: "give until it hurts?"

I suppose it's possible to have a non-percentage standard, but I don't recommend it. In the passage above, Paul said that the offering should be *"a sum of money in keeping with your income."* As previously stated, this offering was not a regular offering, so I wouldn't consider this to be a general command. However, it does evidence the wisdom of giving proportionally.

This is an area where I believe the tithe is very instructive. If God set up a multi-century system for a tax that was proportional, there's a very good reason he did so. If you generate a lot of income, you have a lot to share. If you make less, you have less to give. Proportional giving is fair and just makes sense (Luke 12:48).

LARGE, ONE-TIME OFFERINGS

Because of our heavily monetized world (i.e. everything has a currency value attached to it), it's easy and convenient to think of everything in terms of percentages. It makes sense for many of us to think of our offerings in these terms. But not all types of offerings fall in this paradigm. When the newly baptized believers sold property and possessions to support the early church, their giving was in the form of large, one-time gifts.

It can be difficult to look at New Testament examples to model the specifics of how we might give today, partly because their society was so different. There are many New Testament passages that exemplify and support what appears to be extreme giving. See for example Mark 12:43-44; Acts 2:44-45, 4:32-37, 20:35; 1 Corinthians 9:1-18, 16:1-3; 2 Corinthians 8:1-24, 9:1-15; Galatians 6:6; 1 Timothy 5:3, 17, 6:17-19; and 1 John 3:17-18. In some cases, believers gave their stored savings/family wealth.

I want to provide an example of generous, faithful giving that might fall outside the norm today. Consider an elderly widow who owned two houses, but only had a modest social security income. What if she decided to sell one house and give the money to the church and other charitable causes? What if her plan was to continue to live in other house and live off her social security, but to give only a nominal amount in her weekly offering because of her small income?

Although her continued weekly offering might be very small, she gave a huge one-time offering. I suppose she could have sold the house, kept the money, and slowly distributed it to the church (which is what some might choose to do). Although her offering doesn't fit into the percentage of giving paradigm, it would be a tremendous one-time gift that pleases God and has biblical precedent.

PRE-MEDITATED OFFERINGS

> *Remember this: Whoever sows sparingly will also reap sparingly, and whoever sows generously will also reap generously. Each of you should give what you have decided in your heart to give, not reluctantly or under compulsion, for God loves a cheerful giver. (2 Corinthians 9:6-7)*

Here, Paul urged the Corinthian believers to give what they had decided in their hearts to give. That implies that they needed to take time in advance to think, meditate and pray before deciding what they would give. It was a way to take compulsion out of their giving.

Although deciding what you will give in advance isn't a biblical command, it's a good practice. Most people do this anyway, because they need to write their check before they come to church. Many now give electronically in a way where they have time to quietly consider their offering. Taking the time to consider your offerings is really at the core of what we need to do to have cheerful giving.

SHOULD TAXES AFFECT OUR OFFERINGS?

In other words, should we give the percentage we have decided in our hearts before or after taxes? Well, because there is no set percentage, it is really up to you. Keep in mind that everything taken out of paychecks is meant to benefit you: federal tax, state tax, disability, worker's comp, 401(k), HSA, health and dental insurance, etc. Whatever your philosophy, consider that there's a pretty big difference between giving pre- and post-tax.

Some people live in high-tax socialist countries, where over 50% of their income is taken from their pay. For U.S. taxpayers, starting in 2018, the Congress and President Trump doubled the standard deduction and limited state and local tax itemized deductions. Some are concerned that this may have a chilling effect on charitable giving, because for many this will effectively eliminate the tax deduction incentive for charitable giving (i.e. many will simply use the standard deduction, whether they give charitably or not).

IS OK TO HAVE ACCOUNTABILITY FOR OFFERINGS?

Some churches take pledges or have other means in which members are held accountable for their offerings. Is this wrong? In principle, I would say no, because there's no biblical prohibition to accountability. In fact, accountability in certain forms is critical for our character growth and spiritual well-being (2 Timothy 3:16-17; 1 John 1:5-10). Certainly, God holds everyone accountable (Hebrews 4:13; 1 Peter 1:17).

However, and this is a big however, we should be very careful not to create an atmosphere of compulsion. We shouldn't pressure each other to give reluctantly. From my experience, there's a fine line between challenging someone's faith (Hebrews 10:24-25) and guilting them into giving. Similarly, we don't want to create a boastful atmosphere (Matthew 6:1-4).

Some churches are completely hands-off, when it comes to accountability for giving. Certainly, those churches don't run the risk of producing compulsive or reluctant giving. My concern for groups like that is that its members won't be spurred on in their faith and may not get the help they need financially.

> **Overall, I believe churches have a responsibility to help their members do well spiritually AND financially. The two can be very connected.**

Overall, I believe churches have a responsibility to help their members do well spiritually AND financially. The two can be very connected. If a church expects generous giving but doesn't help its members to do well financially (which connects to many other areas of life), then it can create bitterness in the long run. Churches can do many things to help their members financially like teaching relevant Scriptures, having workshops and promoting character through personal interaction in small groups. Church leaders: do those under your leadership believe you care about their finances?

BREAK DOWN PSYCHOLOGICAL BARRIERS TO GIVING!

If you believe that you should give more generously, but are having a hard time doing it, you may have some psychological barriers holding you back. Here are some barriers and some quick thoughts on how to overcome them.

I can't afford to give the baseline percentage standard I set for myself!

Actually, you can unless you set your standard really high. Think about it: you only give when you make money. What you need to do is figure out a way to cut your expenses. Your devotion, with God's help, will shape you into someone who spends less than you make (see Chapter 2).

I'll start giving after getting out of debt.

If you have income, you should honor God with a portion of it, even if you have debt. I say that with one exception: you shouldn't increase your debt in order to give. If you are buried under high-interest debt and don't make enough money to pay your bills, then you have no money to give. Your solution lies in spending less than you make. If your desire to honor God with an offering, it will help motivate you to get out of debt.

My income is small or inconsistent.

This may be the case for many students and teenagers. Don't

ignore offerings at a young age, because it is such an important time to build your character and convictions. This may also apply to those who own businesses, make commission pay, or have inconsistent schedules. If you don't want to regularly calculate your income, I recommend you look at what your income was over the last three months and use that to determine what you might give on a weekly basis. Then you can adjust it every so often.

If I give, it would be out of compulsion!
If that is truly the case, then you shouldn't give. The better solution is to change your heart about giving. Read the Scriptures, pray about it and get advice from godly people.

I will slowly work up to my goal.
Well, it sounds like you are moving in the right direction. If you have the conviction that you should give a certain amount, then just do it! Step out on faith and watch to see what God does. (See Proverbs 3:9-10).

CONCLUSION
We must all have some kind of standard for honoring God with our wealth that we can stick to. No matter where we are with this, we can all work on our giving, whether in amount or heart. After looking at the Scriptures, you may feel you need to set a new, higher standard for yourself. If so, know that God will be pleased and will help you along!

Chapter 2

Spend Less Than You Make

When my kids were younger, they used to like it when I would quiz them on math. Sometimes, I'd throw in a problem like: "What's 4 minus 5?" Most of the time, I'd catch them off guard. But if my children were paying attention, they'd see that the answer was actually a negative number. If 4 minus 5 reflects your finances, you've got some changes to make.

Spending less than you make is easier said than done! The rule is so simple to understand, but so difficult to follow, because we have to fight our natural instincts to consume. As humans, we have an animal-like nature that has helped us survive as a species for millions of years. We are genetically designed for quick, short-term thinking.

> **Until we figure out how to spend less than we make, we will never grow our wealth.**

Our ancestors quickly recognized the saber-toothed tiger hiding in the bushes and ran to safety.[5] They ate as much as they could when the food was around, because they needed the energy for tomorrow when food might not be available. They jumped to conclusions and it saved their lives. In today's modern world, those natural instincts betray us. We need to look ahead decades, not hours and days.

A recent study found that 60% of Americans are unable to spend less than they make.[6] Until we figure out how to spend less than we make, we will never grow our wealth. Some suffer losses under unfortunate circumstances, but the great majority of people who don't grow their wealth, fail because of their lack of effort.

Lazy hands make for poverty,
  but diligent hands bring wealth.
He who gathers crops in summer is a prudent son,
  but he who sleeps during harvest is a disgraceful son.
(Proverbs 10:4-5)

I picture the modern disgraceful son on the couch snacking and channel surfing. Whether it's not working hard enough or spending too much—we have a problem. The problem is that we will run out of money or, worse yet, get into a bunch of debt.

Budgeting Concept: Discretionary vs. Non-Discretionary Expenses

Non-discretionary expenses are required expenses like rent or mortgage, automobile related expenses, debt payments, medical expenses, etc. Discretionary expenses are expenses you can immediately control, like food, entertainment, vacations, clothing and sundries. When you budget, focus on cutting discretionary expenses, because that is where you will make the most progress.

In our quest to spend less than we make, I do not want to discount our God-given personalities, which color so much of how we perceive spending and saving. For a select few, saving comes naturally. For most, it is incredibly difficult to not spend all their income. Personally, I fall into the later camp. At the end of the month, I often ask myself, "where did all the money go?"

On one hand, we can't excuse our irresponsibility by saying, "This is the way God made me." On the other hand, we shouldn't be too hard on ourselves when we fail. We need to pick ourselves up and keep striving for what we know is right.

THE RULE APPLIES TO EVERYONE

It's big news when celebrities get into financial trouble. We think to ourselves, "How could someone who makes so much money go broke?" We focus on how much money they make, but the real issue is how much money they spend.

According to a study cited by Sports Illustrated in 2009, 78 percent of former NFL players are bankrupt or undergoing severe financial stress within two years of retirement from football, and 60 percent of former NBA players are bankrupt within five years of retirement.[7] If you have the ability to be a pro athlete, maybe you should consider Major League Baseball.

Another media favorite is telling the disaster stories of lottery winners. Their fairy-tale stories almost always end in tragedy. Whenever I hear stories like that, I think of this Scripture:

I have seen a grievous evil under the sun:
wealth hoarded to the harm of its owners,

*or wealth lost through some misfortune,
so that when they have children
there is nothing left for them to inherit.*
(Ecclesiastes 5:13-14)

I'm not picking on celebrities, professional athletes, or lottery winners. I'm only making the point that we are ALL in danger of spending more than we make. Our eyes are bigger than our stomach. It's part of the human condition.

DO YOU WANT TO FEEL RICH OR BE RICH?

Being rich is very different than feeling rich. Being rich is about conserving money, managing money, and letting money work for you, which takes discipline and self-control.

*Those who love pleasure become poor;
those who love wine and luxury will never be rich.*
(Proverbs 21:17 NLT)

Feeling rich is about pleasure, image, and excess, which takes spending and more spending. The fleeting boost you get from feeling rich is a poor substitute for the real thing. The two don't mix well at all. Sure, some people are able to be rich and feel rich, but don't let that confuse you. Make no mistake: keeping up appearances and indulgences (small and large) are the enemy of being rich.

Let me acknowledge that we have a lot working against us. In addition to our primal nature urging us to have short-term thinking, we have advertisers manipulating our minds. Advertising these days is shameless. Sex sells and so does image. It reminds me of this slogan: "Why be you, when you can be new!" (from the movie *Robots*).[8]

> **Make no mistake: keeping up appearances and indulgences (small and large) are the enemy of being rich.**

Advertisers will do just about anything to get our attention. It has gotten to the point where traditional advertising is losing its effect on our desensitized minds. Now, products are conspicuously placed in movies and series to subtly influence us.

It's a common misconception that you need to make a lot of money to build wealth. Building wealth isn't about how much money you make. There are many people who make very little but manage to save and invest. You need to do more than budget; you must follow through on your budget!

If the general populous were honest with itself, it would admit that it was addicted to things and consumables. As a first-world consumer, nothing feels more painful than financial discipline. For most, it's even worse than dieting and exercise!

No discipline seems pleasant at the time, but painful. Later on, however, it produces a harvest of righteousness and peace for those who have been trained by it.
(Hebrews 12:11)

As Christians, we need to spend less than we make and harvest that righteousness and peace! Even though I'm not devoting many pages in this book to this subject, I can't over-emphasize how critical it is. It's the key to unlocking many great things in life, even beyond wealth. When we spend less than we make, we take a big step closer to contentment.

Chapter 3
Aggressively Pay Off Debt

Give to everyone what you owe them: If you owe taxes, pay taxes; if revenue, then revenue; if respect, then respect; if honor, then honor. Let no debt remain outstanding, except the continuing debt to love one another, for whoever loves others has fulfilled the law. (Romans 13:7-8)

Contrary to sound Biblical teaching, our world is soaked in debt. As of early-2019, the U.S.'s national debt had exceeded 22 trillion dollars. Odds are that your state and municipality also have crushing debt loads. According to CNBC, when you remove the top 25 cash-holding corporations, the remaining U.S. corporations have only $0.12 in cash for every $1.00 of debt.[9] The debt ratio for these companies is worse than it was in 2008 during the financial crisis.

Compound interest is the eighth wonder of the world. He who understands it, earns it ...he who doesn't ...pays it.
—Albert Einstein[10]

As of January 2018, the average individual in the U.S. carried over $6,375 in credit card debt.[11] The average household that carries debt carried over $16,800 in credit card debt. Even at a modest 12 percent credit card interest rate, the average household would owe about $175 per month in interest alone!

Most people need to borrow to buy a car, go to college or buy a house. But many also borrow for entertainment, vacations, expensive food and other luxuries. The crazy thing is that at every turn you are encouraged to do so. There's almost something freakish about you if you are "debt free."

We have to pay for just about everything in life. The average Class of 2017 college graduate has $39,400 in student loan debt, up 6 percent from 2016.[12] Many of these students will not pay off their school debt for decades!

MY DEEP DARK DEBT HOLE

I can empathize with those who are in serious debt. I spent the better part of ten years trying to dig my way out of debt. To this day I struggle to fully understand why things happened the way they did for me. Perhaps it was so that I would write this book. Maybe it was to keep my feet on the ground in my relationship with God.

My struggles with money led me to worry and obsess over money and debt. I never thought of myself as that kind of person. That side of me never came out, because I had never had debt before.

After I went to law school, I had only a modest amount of debt. I was fortunate to have had work opportunities and scholarships during my undergraduate years. Also, the law school I went to was moderately priced at the time.

But because I anticipated making decent money as a lawyer, while still in school, I started to spend like I was already making lots of money. I bought a $5,000 laptop, which is like spending $10,000 on a computer today. Ridiculous! I ate out a lot and lived in an apartment that was too expensive for me. Not smart!

Instead of taking one of the job offers I received from the local district attorney's office or law firm, I decided to move to the San Francisco Bay Area on faith. I was asked to take a leadership role in my church's singles ministry on a volunteer basis. By moving, I committed myself to many more months of studying to take another bar exam.

Finding decent work was very difficult. The Bay Area was very expensive (and is even more so now). Despite the challenges, it was truly an exciting and fulfilling time for me. Through my work with church I found the love of my life and we got married. We had great plans and dreams for our lives.

Not soon after, the dot com crash decimated the local economy. Both my wife and I lost our jobs. Then, 9/11 happened, which further hurt the economy. We kept believing things would turn around. We prayed, looked for work, and did whatever freelance work we could find.

In hindsight though, we kept on spending like it was 1999 even when we didn't have jobs. We weren't willing to make major changes to our lifestyle until we finally realized our debt was getting out of control. When it was all said and done, my wife and I racked up almost $100,000 in debt.

Instead of responding wisely to our financial situation, we used credit to buy us time. We were inflexible and not humble to what God was doing in our lives. I felt a deep sense of failure and stress. The stress even caused me to lose part of my eyebrows, a condition called alopecia areata.

> *Submit yourselves, then, to God. Resist the devil, and he will flee from you. Come near to God and he will come near to you. Wash your hands, you sinners, and purify your hearts, you double-minded. Grieve, mourn and wail. Change your laughter to mourning and your joy to gloom. Humble yourselves before the Lord, and he will lift you up.* (James 4:7-10)

Not long after starting to humble ourselves to a lower cost lifestyle, we attend a Biblical financial seminar that truly changed our lives. It was hosted by Greg Garcia (who wrote the foreword). I learned that the way I handle debt is a spiritual matter, not just a practical one. Instead of seeing the numbers, I saw sins in my life like materialism, laziness, and pride.

> *The wicked borrow and do not repay, but the righteous give generously.* (Psalms 37:21)

My wife and I decided to live within our means—no ifs, ands, or buts! For a while, we ate spaghetti or beans and rice almost every day for every meal. We stopped buying gifts completely (yes, even Christmas gifts). We took on extra work. It's amazing how when you make certain painful cuts in your spending, you start to find many other ways to save money. It is almost as if you gain the new super-power of cost cutting.

> **I learned that the way I handle debt is a spiritual matter, not just a practical one.**

The difference in our lives was a true humility toward our situation. We weren't just willing to work hard, we were willing to radically alter our lifestyle. Of course, it worked. More recently, we had to again scale down our lifestyle. We've done it twice now and can do it again if need be. Once you humble yourself to living within your means, your character becomes much more resilient to financial change.

DEBTORS LOVED BY GOD

I realize that dealing with debt can be tremendously demoralizing, because I've been there. We can feel frustrated, trapped, and beaten down by the difficult cycle that debt puts us in. It's easy to get down on yourself, which just makes things worse.

Money coach Tammy Lally defines a condition called "money shame" as "the intensely painful feeling or experience of believing that you're flawed and therefore unworthy of love and belonging based on our bank account balances, our debts, our homes, our cars, and our job title."[13] She and other experts have added a psychological component to their financial counseling, because they've recognized that people's formative beliefs about money is often the root cause of their problems. She recommends openness with our suffering and letting go of our past through surrender, faith, and forgiveness.

I know of no better way to do that than to internalize God's love for us. This is not merely an intellectual exercise, but also an emotional one, which must be done with both God and people. Reach out to God and to others you trust in the faith.

> *He who did not spare his own Son, but gave him up for us all—how will he not also, along with him, graciously give us all things? Who will bring any charge against those whom God has chosen? It is God who justifies. Who then is the one who condemns? No one. Christ Jesus who died—more than that, who was raised to life—is at the right hand of God and is also interceding for us. Who shall separate us from the love of Christ? Shall trouble or hardship or persecution or famine or nakedness or danger or sword?* (Romans 8:32-35)

Being a debtor doesn't make you any less loved by God. Christ still willingly died for you and does not condemn you. Don't let the *"trouble or hardship"* of debt separate you from the love of Christ. Tackling debt takes a lot of discipline and tough love on yourself (and maybe from others), so keep your chin up!

A LITTLE HELP FROM A FRIEND

> *Better is open rebuke*
> *than hidden love.*
> *Wounds from a friend can be trusted,*
> *but an enemy multiplies kisses.* (Proverbs 27:5-6)

Sometimes, we need others in our life to help us get in touch with our own greed. Back when I was neck deep in debt, a good friend at church asked me to help him move on a Saturday morning. After grabbing my morning latte, I stopped in to get a deluxe car wash. I arrived at the move about ninety minutes late, hoping no one would notice.

Right as I pulled up in my shiny car, my friend, who knew about my financial challenges, chastised me for getting the car wash. I tried to justify the decision by saying it was a good deal, but of course my friend was right. Truth be told, I was much more embarrassed that I had showed up late to help him move.

> Some of us are content with a plan to slowly reduce our debt. The Bible, however, tells us to take an extreme view toward paying off debt.

Somehow, that whole ugly situation got me in touch with my greed and really helped me to repent. Ironically, the situation resulted in giving me spiritual power. It wasn't exactly like Ebenezer Scrooge in *A Christmas Carol*, but it was a turning point for me.[14] Will you listen when someone tries to talk some sense into you? What friend can you help out with a loving rebuke?

Most of us tend to be very closed off when it comes to talking about our finances. It's the one area in life that others rarely see. We need to get it out in the open and talk to others!

ARE YOU SERIOUS ABOUT PAYING OFF DEBT?

Some of us don't even want to tally up our own debt, because we fear the truth. Ignorance is bliss, but ignorance has terrible consequences. If we face the truth, we can get alarmed about debt, angry at debt and serious about paying it off (2 Corinthians 7:10-11).

Some of us are content with a plan to slowly reduce our debt. The Bible, however, tells us to take an extreme view toward paying off debt.

> *My son, if you have put up security for your neighbor,*
> *if you have shaken hands in pledge for a stranger,*
> *you have been trapped by what you said,*
> *ensnared by the words of your mouth.*
> *So do this, my son, to free yourself,*
> *since you have fallen into your neighbor's hands:*

> *Go—to the point of exhaustion—*
> *and give your neighbor no rest!*
> *Allow no sleep to your eyes,*
> *no slumber to your eyelids.*
> *Free yourself, like a gazelle from the hand of the hunter,*
> *like a bird from the snare of the fowler.*
> (Proverbs 6:1-5)

This passage talks about being a cosigner (a surety) on a potentially bad loan. That tells you something about cosigning on loans: don't do it. However you got into debt, don't rest until you get out of it!

> *Do not be one who shakes hands in pledge*
> *or puts up security for debts;*
> *if you lack the means to pay,*
> *your very bed will be snatched from under you.*
> (Proverbs 22:26-27)

Do what it takes to pay your debts. Cut your expenses drastically. Increase your income if possible. Refinance your debt to a lower interest rate. Pray and humble yourself to God and he will lift you up.

BANKRUPTCY FOR CHRISTIANS?

Bankruptcy is a complex issue for Christians. Many Christians believe it's wrong for them because they are failing to pay back money they borrowed. Personally, I do not feel so strongly about that, since bankruptcy is a legitimate part of our legal system and has roots in the Old Testament practice of periodic debt forgiveness. Also, investors routinely use bankruptcy as a legitimate means of minimizing risks by investing in corporate entities.

That being said, my concern would be for the character of the person filing bankruptcy. If you wipe your debts away without changing your character, you are likely to repeat your mistakes. I believe bankruptcy is inappropriate for Christians in most situations, but in extreme circumstances it can be useful.

The scope of bankruptcy protection has been reduced over the years, so you might be surprised to learn it is not available in some situations. Rather than wiping out all of your debt, you may only qualify for a Chapter 13 bankruptcy, where you participate in a court-administered debt repayment plan.

WHAT'S THE DIFFERENCE BETWEEN "CONSUMER DEBT," "BAD DEBT," AND "GOOD DEBT?"

> *Money is a new and terrible form of slavery, and, like the old form of personal slavery, it corrupts both the slave and the slave-owner, but it is even worse because it frees the slave-owner from personal relations.* —Leo Tolstoy[15]

"Bad debt" refers to debt that you got into for "bad" reasons. So, credit card and personal loans are typically considered bad debt. "Consumer debt" is basically the same thing. It refers to purchases that are consumed, so to speak, where you have nothing to show for it. Traditionally, home loans, car loans and school loans are typically considered "good debt."

There may have been a time when those labels were generally true, but that time has long since passed. Nowadays, there are all sorts of homes, cars and educations that have an extreme luxury factor. They are less of a tool and more of an indulgence. On the other hand, someone might use a credit card to pay rent and buy groceries.

The truth is that debt is just debt, regardless of how you got it. That's not to say it doesn't matter why you got into debt. But at the end of the day, it is just a number you must pay off.

Legally speaking, you have secured and unsecured debt. Secured debt allows a creditor to take back collateral if you default, like a car or home. Unsecured debt requires a debtor to collect judgments through the court system. It's better to owe unsecured debt than secured debt, because you have more leeway in how to resolve it.

> **Bad debt is high-interest debt. You can basically rank your debts from bad to worse by looking at the interest rate. A high rate of interest on your debt turns you into a hamster on a wheel.**

Bad debt is high-interest debt. You can basically rank your debts from bad to worse by looking at the interest rate. A high rate of interest on your debt turns you into a hamster on a wheel. You run and run but get nowhere. That's where your creditors want you.

Even for so-called "good debt," there are some cases where paying off high-interest car loans, student loans, and home loans should be your priority. In a relatively low-interest rate environment like we've had since 2008, it's easy to refinance most debts if you have a decent credit rating. But if you can't refinance, your surest way to get ahead is to pay off the high-interest debt first before investing.

If you've already "invested" in that car, home or education consider the interest rate you are paying on the debt. If the rate is above 4-6 percent on the so-called "good debt," get advice from someone good with money about whether you should treat it like "bad debt."

SOME PRACTICALS ON DEALING WITH DEBT

1. Dealing with debt can be very stressful. Don't underestimate the toll it can take on you emotionally. Be sure to talk to others about what you are going through and get encouragement (Hebrews 3:12-13).

2. Think, pray and get advice before getting into any big debt (Proverbs 15:22). Sometimes, we can make big decisions without fully appreciating the consequences. The price tag on big ticket items have gone up dramatically in recent years: homes, cars, educations, etc. Getting into debt happens very quickly. Paying it off happens very slowly.

3. Get psyched! Watch TV shows or read books on paying off debt. Team up with friends who are doing the same thing. Consider joining or forming a debt support group. Treat each debt payment with joy and excitement!

Chapter 4
SAVE

Saving is not just a to-do on a checklist. It's actually a way of life that takes special discipline beyond paying off debt. The reason for saving is simple: you'll need the money for things like unexpected expenses, periods of unemployment, helping children through college and retirement. You need to save consistently over a lifetime, or it doesn't really work.

> *Dishonest money dwindles away,*
> *   but whoever gathers money little by little makes it grow.* (Proverbs 13:11)

There are at least two reasons why wealth grows *"little by little"*. First, most people never come into large chunks of money to save. When you consistently save, time can make up for modest means. Second, you value your savings much more when you work long and hard for it. It helps you not to spend too much. When money comes easily or dishonestly, it's spent just as easily.

THE HUMAN TENDENCY TO UNDERESTIMATE FUTURE EXPENSES

Saving large sums of money takes more discipline than paying off debt. That first $5,000 you save sure could buy a lot of little luxuries! Or maybe it could be a down payment on that new car you've been eyeing. Do savings burn holes in your pockets?

You may say, "But isn't money for spending? Shouldn't you be able spend if you can afford it and are not in debt?" Yes, but you shouldn't spend it all!

> *Go to the ant, you sluggard;*
> *   consider its ways and be wise!*
> *It has no commander,*
> *   no overseer or ruler,*
> *yet it stores its provisions in summer*
> *   and gathers its food at harvest*
> *How long will you lie there, you sluggard?*

*When will you get up from your sleep?
A little sleep, a little slumber,
    a little folding of the hands to rest—
and poverty will come on you like a thief
    and scarcity like an armed man.* (Proverbs 6:6-10)

Have you ever been robbed before? Me neither, but let's imagine it for a second. A large man holding a pistol has just kicked in your back door! All you can really do is give him your valuables and hope he doesn't shoot you. Lord knows we need a good scare to get us to start saving!

Why do we take it easy and not save when we know we have never-ending expenses? I think many of us trick ourselves into believing that we have enough, but we haven't taken an honest look at our future expenses. We don't take into account inflation and far-off expenses. We ignore predictable "emergencies" like family health costs and auto repairs. We incorrectly assume we will always make at least as much money as we are making today.

> **Who will provide for you when you are in need, because you saved nothing?**

Unlike most of us, the ant naturally saves. It doesn't need someone to command it or nag it to store up food. It doesn't stress out or have to psych itself into saving. It's just part of what it is. Let's become like the ant: a hard-worker and routine saver.

SHOULD WE FEEL GUILTY ABOUT SAVING MONEY?

No, not all! It's not unspiritual or worldly. Who will provide for you when you are you need, because you saved nothing? Are you expecting others to work hard and save to provide for you, so you can take it easy? That's not godly. How can we give to others if we spend all our income on ourselves? Now that's downright unspiritual!

Although we could give to others anytime we have some money, most of us won't feel great about giving if we don't have a solid base of savings. I'm not talking about saving huge sums, but I am talking about being prepared for predictable, routine future expenses you know are coming around. Let's face it, we need to feel great about our personal financial situation, before we can feel great about consistently helping others.

YOUR LAST TEST BEFORE INVESTING: SAVE AN EMERGENCY FUND

Even with the improvement in financial outlook, however, 40 percent still say they cannot cover a $400 emergency expense, or would do so by borrowing or selling something.
—Federal Reserve Board's Report on the Economic Well-Being of U.S. Households in 2017[16]

The wise store up choice food and olive oil, but fools gulp theirs down. (Proverbs 21:20)

An "emergency fund" is just a sensational name for having some cash savings. It's not just for emergencies, but really for anything that comes up. In my mind, this is the last test you must past before you are ready to invest.

Why have it when you can just use a credit card if you get into a jam? Why have it when you could begin investing the money right away? Well, in theory you can skip over saving an emergency fund, but I strongly warn against skipping it.

There are a lot of practical reasons to have it, but I think the main benefit is a psychological one. For most people or families, it will be a sizeable pool of cash. You have to have the discipline to not spend it. Your mind has to be in the right place. It is a constant reminder that anything can happen.

Tip: Don't put all your extra money into you 401(k) or IRA! Keep some in cash! If you are bent on investing with it, there is a way to have your cake and eat it too when it comes to emergency funds. You can put money into a ROTH IRA; the invested amounts that can be retrieved without penalty. You can invest those funds without paying tax on the gains. For ROTH 401(k)s, be watchful of your company's withdrawal rules.

How big should your emergency fund be? Experts agree that you should have a minimum of at least 3 months' worth of your normal expenses. Many experts advocate you should have a 6-month, 9-month, or even one-year emergency fund!

Rather than arbitrarily picking a number of months, I advise you to honestly evaluate your personal risk factors to decide how much you should save. What's the job market like in your field? For families: are you dual-income or single-income? Do you have children or others to support? Are there any other unusual risk factors you might have like medical issues? The more unstable your situation or higher your fixed expenses are, the more you want in your emergency fund.

A BRIEF NOTE ABOUT MARITAL UNITY AND FINANCES

> *'For this reason a man will leave his father and mother and be united to his wife, and the two will become one flesh'? So they are no longer two, but one flesh. Therefore what God has joined together, let no one separate.*
> (Matthew 19:5-6 quoting Genesis 2:24)

Soon after my wife and I were married, we would spend regular time with a couple in our church who lived a few blocks away. They would patiently listen to our disagreements and differences of opinion, but never took sides, which sometimes frustrated us. Their counsel was very humbling, because they would always point out to us that it was more important to be unified than to be right.

Our instinctive quest to change each other's point of view, became our spiritual quest to understand and value each other's point of view. We learned that if we wanted to have a successful marriage, we had to give up doing things our own way. Of course, we still have our own opinions, but we are now focused on being unified. We are very grateful for the counsel we received, because it has really helped all aspects of our marriage, including how we handle our money.

It doesn't surprise me to hear money is the number one cause of stress in marriage and divorce. Money touches every area of our lives and can sharply expose our differing values. I view the stress not coming from money itself, but rather the differing values that it can represent. Some of those differences can have lifelong implications and be relentlessly frustrating. Rather than fight over the details of handling money, I strongly suggest exploring each other's deep-seated beliefs and feelings in a respectful manner.

Serious mishandling of money can easily destroy precious marital trust. Don't do it! "It's better to be poor than a liar." (Proverbs 19:22b). You definitely don't want to be both. There's so much to say on this subject, but I won't, because I would really be talking more about marriage than money. There are tons of great books about marriage. There are even some specifically devoted to marriage and money.

I just want to discuss two specific issues. First, I want to emphasize that saving money and having a solid emergency fund is good for a marriage. Although it might be stressful at first to discuss financial issues, to budget and to curb spending, it ultimately builds unity and reduces stress.

A "survey conducted by the market research firm Synovate, shows that people who follow three basic practices of wise money management—maintain an adequate emergency fund, don't carry a balance on credit cards, and use a budget to guide spending decisions—are less stressed about their finances than most people."[17] "Households with 6 or more months' worth of living expenses in an emergency fund were the least likely…to report feeling stressed over their household's finances."

Second, I want to say that joint accounts versus separate accounts is not the key issue. The important issue is unity. It is critical that you are open, transparent, and work together on your finances. I personally believe that as people who believe in God's version of marriage, you 100% share your lives and your finances.

Typically, having a joint checking account is the sensible solution for fostering financial unity. If a couple felt uncomfortable with having every transaction potentially monitored by their spouse, they could have separate accounts for their personal discretionary spending, in addition to their joint account for paying regular expenses. There could certainly be other setups that might work for you.

RECAP

How are you doing with the Four Rules of Spiritual Finances? Do you:

1. Honor God with your wealth?
2. Spend less than you make?
3. Aggressively pay off bad debt?
4. Save?

I realize that it may take you many years to get these rules down. Like with me, it may take you a decade or more. Don't give up! Don't take shortcuts!

> *Son though he was, he learned obedience from what he suffered and, once made perfect, he became the source of eternal salvation for all who obey him.* (Hebrews 5:8-9)

Even Jesus needed to learn obedience through suffering. Like Jesus, God is perfecting you through hardship. Humble yourself before God, and he will lift you up in due time.

Section II:

BIBLICAL PERSPECTIVES ON WEALTH

Many Christians dismiss wealth as a topic of less importance than topics like faith, evangelism, sexual purity and love. Yet, Jesus and his apostles extensively taught about wealth. The Old Testament is also rife with teaching on the subject. Possibly for cultural reasons, wealth is an often-neglected subject in our sermons, group discussions and personal study.

"You cannot serve both God and money." (Matthew 6:24b)

How we handle our wealth says a lot about us. If you really think about it, wealth is just an extension of ourselves. It's often said that wealth amplifies our true selves, whether good or bad. Understanding the proper role of wealth in our lives is critical to our relationship with God.

The Bible employs many perspectives on wealth—each addressing important issues that we regularly deal with in life. If we are to grow as followers of Jesus, it's critical that we have a biblical mindset about wealth. It will mean the difference between your greatness, mediocrity or even failure spiritually.

Chapter 5
From Slave to Slave Master

Congratulations! You've done it! You've learned to: 1) honor God with your wealth, 2) spend less than you make, 3) pay off your debt, and 4) save. Now what?

Albeit subtle, this is a turning point in your life. There aren't flashing lights. There's no great celebration to mark the occasion. Nobody congratulated you. Odds are nobody knew. You might not even have realized it, but it is a very important benchmark.

> *The rich rule over the poor,*
> *and the borrower is slave to the lender.* (Proverbs 22:7)

You've gone from being a slave to your creditors, to being a creditor yourself.[18] Although you may still have a "good debt" mortgage or a car loan, you now have money to invest. How does investing make you a master? For example, if you take $100 and buy a share of a company's stock, you are an owner (a master). Similarly, if you give $100 towards helping the poor, others work to service the poor (as directed by you).

When you had bad debt, it was wise for you to focus on paying it off. It wouldn't have made sense to put your money into an investment, while simultaneously paying high interest. Your decision was simple: if you have extra money, pay off your debt!

Now what do you do with your disposable income? You could spend it all on consumer goods, which would be a horrible idea. Odds are that if you've made it this far, you're ready to focus on the next steps.

FINANCIAL FREEDOM?

The concept of "financial freedom" is often used to describe a way of life where you have enough money to do what you want. Although the Bible advises us to be free from debt, which enslaves us, having a lot of money can also enslave us. These concepts are discussed throughout this book, but I wanted to address the terminology here. Let me divide the idea of financial freedom into two categories: worldly financial freedom and spiritual financial freedom.

Worldly financial freedom is not a true freedom, which can only come from within. It's nice to have a lot of money, but it doesn't free us from what truly enslaves us (John 8:31-36). Setting a goal of worldly financial freedom can easily lead to a life of greed and compromise. Get rich quick schemes sometimes use the "financial freedom" terminology. It conjures up a false sense of untapped wisdom.

> Worldly financial freedom is not a true freedom, which can only come from within. It's nice to have a lot of money, but it doesn't free us from what truly enslaves us.

Spiritual financial freedom, as I define it, is not allowing money and wealth to hinder your relationship with God. To do that, you must bend money to God's will rather than allowing money to lead you away from God. You don't have to be rich to achieve spiritual financial freedom. Anyone can achieve it at any time, if you put into practice the word of God.

THE ISRAELITES' DIFFICULT TRANSITION TO FREEDOM

God used Moses, Aaron, and many severe plagues to break the Israelites out of slavery in Egypt. Instead of trusting God and what he was doing in their lives, they were inclined to play it safe and go back to slavery in Egypt (Exodus 14:11-12). After being oppressed for so many generations, they couldn't believe what was happening. They couldn't see that the God of their fathers wanted them to have better lives.

God truly unleashed his power with mega-miracles like the parting of the Red Sea and the Pillar of Fire. With those and other miracles, God put an exclamation point on his statement of freedom and love for his people. But did the Israelites enjoy their new-found freedom? Sadly, not very much and not for very long.

> *In the desert the whole community grumbled against Moses and Aaron. The Israelites said to them, "If only we had died by the LORD's hand in Egypt! There we sat around pots of meat and ate all the food we wanted, but you have brought us out into this desert to starve this entire assembly to death." (Exodus 16:2-3)*

I don't think the Israelites really wish they had died, but they were in a new and uncomfortable situation. They hated being oppressed by the Egyptians, but that was all they knew. While being faced with putting their absolute trust in Yahweh in the desert, their recollection of Egypt brightened. Instead of hard labor and infant killings, they remembered filling up on *"pots of meat."*

Having and maintaining wealth has a culture of its own. Some of it is good and some of it is bad. We want to embrace the good parts of it and reject the bad. Transitioning to a different mindset about the handling of wealth can be challenging and take time.

Like the Israelites in Moses' day, we can crave the simpler existence of borrowing, spending and slaving to pay back the debt. What more could you want than a full stomach and Netflix? Instead of making the transition, we can easily stay in the mindset of a slave. Money can bring us a level of freedom, but we must also accept the accompanying responsibility investing carries.

> *For the LORD your God will bless you as he has promised, and you will lend to many nations but will borrow from none. You will rule over many nations but none will rule over you.* (Deuteronomy 15:6)

I like God's plan for his people in the Promised Land. He didn't have his people escape complete slavery in Egypt only to get into debt slavery in the Promised Land. If that were the case, it wouldn't be much of a promised land. It is fascinating to me that in the same chapter, God instructs his people to regularly cancel debts (i.e. not have a debt-based society) and provide for the poor. Society today could learn a thing or two from the Israelite society.

Even the New Testament discusses the idea of getting out of slavery.

> *Were you a slave when you were called? Don't let it trouble you—although if you can gain your freedom, do so. For the one who was a slave when called to faith in the Lord is the Lord's freed person; similarly, the one who was free when called is Christ's slave. You were bought at a price; do not become slaves of human beings.* (1 Corinthians 7:21-23)

While you can follow God at any station in life, it's better to do so as a free person. By enslaving yourself with debt, you compromise your slavery to Christ. If you are heavily in debt, don't let it get you down. Take action!

The new world of investing can be very uncomfortable if you are not used to it. It requires you to choose where you want to invest your capital and to oversee it. It may take a while to get used to. The freedom to roam in uncharted financial territory is a whole new phase of your life.

The real question is: what does God want us to do with our money? We know he wants us to honor him with our wealth. We know he wants us to pay off our bad debt. But beyond that, the world opens, and the choices become numerous and overwhelming. Before we talk in specifics about options for investing our wealth (Section III), let us look at the wealth principles in his word and ask him for wisdom in faith (James 1:5).

Chapter 6
Mastering Mammom

Just when we think we've climbed to the top of the mountain, we reach the peak only to see another peak in the distance. We may have finally reached the point where money is working for us, but the real challenge has just begun.

"Do not store up for yourselves treasures on earth, where moths and vermin destroy, and where thieves break in and steal. But store up for yourselves treasures in heaven, where moths and vermin do not destroy, and where thieves do not break in and steal. For where your treasure is, there your heart will be also.

"The eye is the lamp of the body. If your eyes are healthy, your whole body will be full of light. But if your eyes are unhealthy, your whole body will be full of darkness. If then the light within you is darkness, how great is that darkness!" (Matthew 6:19-23)

Jesus lets us in on a little investing secret: treasures in heaven are the most secure investments you can make. If you open your account today, you can also get a free lamp for your body! God credits our account for things like giving to the needy, praying and fasting, but only when done in faith (Matthew 6:4, 6, 18). How's your Bank of Heaven account doing?

Jesus warns us that a stingy spirit fills our body with darkness. The Greek for "healthy" and "unhealthy" in this passage implies generosity and stinginess, respectively (NIV footnotes to Matthew 6:22, 23). When we don't have faith in heaven, we naturally look to earth and its treasures for security and comfort.

> **Jesus warns us that a stingy spirit fills our body with darkness.**

"No one can serve two masters; for either he will hate

the one and love the other, or else he will be loyal to the one and despise the other. You cannot serve God and mammon." (Matthew 6:24 NKJV)

Jesus makes it clear: in the long run, it's impossible to serve two masters. The masters' priorities will conflict. Our hearts will eventually hate the effect one master has on us and love the other. Over time, we tend to side with one or the other. Which will it be for you?

WHAT IN THE WORLD IS MAMMON?

The word "mammon" essentially means wealth. Mammon is the English translation of the Latin word mammona (the King James Bible was based on Latin translations).[19] The word is originally Aramaic, possibly with ancient Hebrew or Syrian roots. Although there was no Syrian god named mammon, Jesus chose to personify mammon as a master that can be served.

1909 painting: The Worship of Mammon by Evelyn De Morgan

During the Middle Ages mammon was commonly personified as the demon of wealth and greed. Mammon has shown up in many writings, including that of Thomas Aquinas, John Milton (*Paradise Lost*), and in modern culture as well. Because of the threat wealth poses to our soul, it is perhaps fitting that mammon be given true demonic status.

Put to death, therefore, whatever belongs to your earthly nature: sexual immorality, impurity, lust, evil desires and greed, which is idolatry. (Colossians 3:5)

Thinking of wealth as a false god may actually be helpful in bringing to life this very real threat. So, am I saying wealth is evil? No, of course not. It's the greed that is idolatry. God created wealth for us to enjoy, but it must have its proper place in our lives. It must be mastered, not worshipped.

HOW DO I MASTER MAMMON?

You master mammon by choosing to have a heavenly focus each and every day. That's the only place mammon has no power.

As the old saying goes, "You can't take it with you!" There's no silver bullet to kill mammon. Dealing with wealth in our lives is a lifelong war that requires many plans of attack.

If we look at society at large, we see it wholeheartedly embracing mammon. The worship of wealth is in full swing. Our whole society relies on it. Even after 9/11, President George W. Bush encouraged Americans to "go shopping more." Boy did Americans go for it, racking up record debt and houses they could not afford. While that contributed to the 2008 financial crisis, I believe the spiritual crisis is the larger story.

> *Do not love this world nor the things it offers you, for when you love the world, you do not have the love of the Father in you. For the world offers only a craving for physical pleasure, a craving for everything we see, and pride in our achievements and possessions. These are not from the Father, but are from this world. And this world is fading away, along with everything that people crave. But anyone who does what pleases God will live forever. (1 John 2:15-17 NLT)*

It's easy to dismiss the whole struggle against mammon out of hand. However, the Scripture above shows us the battle is very real. Materialism and greed are very hard to see, especially when everyone around us is neck deep in them. Maybe we think that greed is only for rich people – and that we aren't rich enough to be greedy. There are many ways to convince ourselves that there is no battle against mammon (or Satan for that matter).

> *So convenient a thing to be a reasonable creature, since it enables one to find or make a reason for every thing one has a mind to do.* —Benjamin Franklin

AM I RICH? IF SO, WHAT DOES THAT MEAN?

We like to think of ourselves as "middle class." In fact, nine out of ten Americans consider themselves middle class, but only 47% are. We associate being middle-class with being hard-working, honest and down-to-earth.[20]

No one wants to be considered "lower class." By the same token, many wealthy people don't like to consider themselves "upper class." It brings to mind arrogance, privilege and greed. Whatever our true status, we want to think of ourselves in the best light.

We've all heard about how much wealthier first-world citizens are than those living in the third world. In that sense, even the poorest of us is rich. Sorry preachers, I don't think those comparisons really do much to change our thinking or behavior. Most of us are out of touch with the poverty in our own cities and towns, much less the poverty in the third world.

> The Bible calls everyone to honor God and be generous, not just "the rich."

I believe our preoccupation with whether we are considered "rich" or not is an unhealthy pursuit. It can't be easily defined and is very subjective. The Bible calls *everyone* to honor God and be generous, not just "the rich." Let's not waste energy engaging in comparing ourselves to our society or even other Christians. Whether we have two small copper coins or a vast empire, having a spiritual mindset about our lives makes us feel rich, which in turn makes us generous.

HOW MUCH IS ENOUGH?

> *Whoever loves money never has enough;*
> *whoever loves wealth is never satisfied with their income.*
> *This too is meaningless.*
> *As goods increase,*
> *so do those who consume them.*
> *And what benefit are they to the owners*
> *except to feast their eyes on them?* (Ecclesiastes 5:10-11)

If we love money, we can never have enough. Increasing our income at the expense of other important things in life has diminishing returns, and I'm not just talking about taxes. You can only consume so much and there are always plenty of people around to help you spend your money as you accumulate it. The pursuit of wealth for the sake of wealth ultimately leaves us empty.

WHEN WILL WE BECOME GENEROUS?

Generosity is a condition of the heart, and very difficult to measure in specific actions or amounts. It can be expressed in many ways. How you give is perhaps as important as how much you give.

While an act of generosity is a simple and beautiful thing, knowing if you are a generous person is not so clear.

The biblical benchmark is whether *"your eyes are healthy,"* filling *"your whole body ... [with] light."* (Matthew 6:22). But, you can't just wink and smile your way into healthy eyes club. Anyone can put on a happy face. You must give to be generous to have your light shine from the inside. It takes real faith and real sacrifice.

Some of us have a goal in our heart about the kind of generosity we want to show. Perhaps it is increasing what you give to your church, to the poor or to friends in need. Perhaps your goal is associated more with your attitude in giving, which may require you to change up how you give. Perhaps it is both. If your conscience is gnawing at you, don't ignore it!

Most of us are natural procrastinators. We can hold back until we achieve a certain self-created benchmark of wealth, before we'll seriously give to God or others. In other words, we've created an obstacle for our generosity. Chances are you'll continue to raise your benchmark or find some other reason to continue to hold back.

Here's an example. Daniel tells himself that he'll start giving a portion of his income to the needy when his 401(k) reaches $100,000 in value. He's thirty years old when he makes the goal and finally reaches that benchmark when he is forty years old. But at forty, he's married and has two children and is focused on the upkeep of his family. He then tells himself he'll start giving to the poor when his 401(k) reaches $250,000.

If we're doing something like this, we're only fooling ourselves, because the issue is a spiritual one and can only be solved spiritually. We need to pray, decide and act! Wouldn't it be better for Daniel if he just started giving something small to the needy at age thirty? Wouldn't that be better for his heart and shape him into a generous person by the time he was forty? If we are able to give, the time to start is now!

Start honoring God with your wealth and being generous to others now. Start with anything but start now! Being generous is like a muscle, you have got to work it out to make it strong. Make it a lifestyle choice like eating healthy and exercising. Trust me, you won't wake up one day and become generous. It is a repetitive decision, that eventually becomes your character. Remember, God isn't looking at amounts, but at the heart.

Chapter 7

Custodians of Wealth

WHOSE MONEY IS IT, ANYWAY?

> The earth is the LORD's, and everything in it,
> the world, and all who live in it. (Psalm 24:1)

> "The silver is mine and the gold is mine," declares the LORD Almighty. (Haggai 2:8 see also 1 Chronicles 29:11)

The idea that God owns the world's wealth is a strange and abstract concept for modern people. Most first world citizens have a very strong sense of personal property ownership, which is a basic tenet of our societies. Even most of the "communist" world has latched onto individualistic thinking, where their citizens are also encouraged to accumulate as much wealth as possible. Our societies feed into our selfish, materialistic tendencies.

Our strong, modern sense of individual wealth ownership is partly a learned, cultural phenomenon. It manifested itself in documents like the *Magna Carta* (1215 A.D.), which protected basic human rights including freedom from excessive government control and property ownership. After centuries of development and refining, our sense of property ownership is well established.

From the time of mankind's creation, God gave us dominion over animals, plants, and the earth (Genesis 1:26-30). That is not to say that he approves of whatever we want to do with our resources. If you were God, how you would want humans to manage their wealth? What about your children: would you want them to squander what you give them or produce even more? Would you want them to share?

BUT I WORKED SO HARD FOR MY WEALTH; IT SHOULD BE ALL MINE!

> You may say to yourself, "My power and the strength of my hands have produced this wealth for me." But remember the LORD your God, for it is he who gives you the ability

to produce wealth, and so confirms his covenant, which he swore to your ancestors, as it is today. (Deuteronomy 8:17-19)

It's easy to justify holding onto our wealth, because we've been skillful and worked hard. But our skill and even our ability to work hard come from God. We've done well to work hard, but we have to keep in mind that the wealth is still God's. As discussed below, God will reward us for what we have done in due time.

WELL DONE, GOOD AND FAITHFUL SERVANT?

Let's carefully read the full "Parable of the Bags of Gold."

"Again, it will be like a man going on a journey, who called his servants and entrusted his wealth to them. To one he gave five bags of gold, to another two bags, and to another one bag, each according to his ability. Then he went on his journey. The man who had received five bags of gold went at once and put his money to work and gained five bags more. So also, the one with two bags of gold gained two more. But the man who had received one bag went off, dug a hole in the ground and hid his master's money.

"After a long time the master of those servants returned and settled accounts with them. The man who had received five bags of gold brought the other five. 'Master,' he said, 'you entrusted me with five bags of gold. See, I have gained five more.'

"His master replied, 'Well done, good and faithful servant! You have been faithful with a few things; I will put you in charge of many things. Come and share your master's happiness!'

"The man with two bags of gold also came. 'Master,' he said, 'you entrusted me with two bags of gold; see, I have gained two more.'

"His master replied, 'Well done, good and faithful servant! You have been faithful with a few things; I will put you in charge of many things. Come and share your master's happiness!'

"Then the man who had received one bag of gold came. 'Master,' he said, 'I knew that you are a hard man,

harvesting where you have not sown and gathering where you have not scattered seed. So I was afraid and went out and hid your gold in the ground. See, here is what belongs to you.'

"His master replied, 'You wicked, lazy servant! So you knew that I harvest where I have not sown and gather where I have not scattered seed? Well then, you should have put my money on deposit with the bankers, so that when I returned I would have received it back with interest.

"'So take the bag of gold from him and give it to the one who has ten bags. For whoever has will be given more, and they will have an abundance. Whoever does not have, even what they have will be taken from them. And throw that worthless servant outside, into the darkness, where there will be weeping and gnashing of teeth.'" (Matthew 25:14-30)

Many of us know this as the "Parable of the Talents."[21] A talent was an ancient measure of weight ranging between 57-130 pounds.[22] In this newer NIV translation, the Greek word "talent" has been translated into "bags of gold." The new terminology makes the situation a little clearer for the modern reader.

At $1,300 per ounce, a talent of gold would be worth somewhere between $890,000 and $2,028,000 today. The footnote in the current New International Version says that "A talent was worth about 20 years of a day laborer's wage." Holy smokes! For the sake of discussion, I'm going to estimate that a modern "bag" or "talent" is worth about $900,000 today.

So, the servants received $4.5M, $1.8M, and $900k in today's dollars, respectively. I find it interesting that those amounts are a fair range of what people today might earn over their lifetimes. Some earn less than others, and God doesn't have a problem with that. It is, after all, God who dispenses the talents or bags of gold.

Jesus could have easily chosen in the parable to make the 5-talent servant the *"wicked, lazy"* servant. It doesn't matter how many talents we have. What matters is how we use them! Perhaps Jesus chose the 1-talent servant to be *"wicked, lazy,"* to make clear that no one is exempt from the Master's judgment, even those who earn less.

I've always heard this passage preached in the context of using and developing our various talents for God. I've never heard this preached in the context of financial giving or investing. Perhaps that's because of the old name "Parable of the Talents," or because there are so many other Scriptures to choose from about financial giving. Is Jesus talking about money or personal talents in the parable?

When we hear the word "talent," we tend to think of talent show skills like singing, dancing, magic or acrobatics. Maybe we think of athletics or academic skill. In the context of the church, talents might include preaching, serving, organizing, counseling, music or outreach.

However, on its face, the parable is talking about investing money (in the form of gold). The Master expected the servants to somehow grow the initial investments of gold. Personally, I think the parable applies to *both* money and our talents. I believe God expects us to grow our wealth and cultivate our talents. To say that this passage is not talking about money, would be very hard to support.

The distinction is really a false dilemma. In many ways, there's little difference between our talents and our money. Talent produces income. That income can be used to advance the gospel. Of course, your talents can be used to directly advance the gospel. We have a responsibility to grow and use both.

BIBLICAL MODEL FOR WEALTH OWNERSHIP

So, if we really don't own anything, that makes us custodians of what's in our possession. Generally speaking, a custodian is someone who looks after or cares for something. The Parable reflects the highest standard of a custodial relationship, which in modern terms would be called a fiduciary relationship. A fiduciary is "a person to whom property or power is entrusted for the benefit of another."

A fiduciary is expected to be extremely loyal to the person for whom he or she owes the duty (called a principal). There must be no conflict of interest between a fiduciary and a principal. Some examples include attorney-client, doctor-patient and agent-principal relationships. So, what does all this really mean?

First and foremost, we are expected to take on the master's priorities when it comes to handling his wealth. One of his priorities is multiplying the wealth he gives us. The rest of the Bible gives us ample direction as to what he wants us to do with what he has given us.

Secondly, we are expected to work hard. The Parable shows us that our motivation to do work comes from our view of God. Do we view him as a *"hard man"* who is undeserving of our service? Do we see him as unfair, because we fail to see how God is investing in us?

Or do we have an eager attitude, considering it an honor to serve the Master?

When you realize you don't work for Me, Inc. anymore, but rather God, Inc., it opens the door to a different kind of thinking. Giving wealth away is a job well done, not a painful exercise in self-denial. As an employee at God, Inc., you've got a company house or apartment, company car and an expense account! You get paid vacation on the garden spot of the universe: planet earth. There's also a golden parachute retirement plan.

> When you realize you don't work for Me, Inc. anymore, but rather God, Inc., it opens the door to a different kind of thinking.

God, Inc. has an unusual corporate culture. You are evaluated on your heart, not your results. So, if your investment results aren't so stellar, you won't get in trouble. He controls the results anyway. You just take what God has given you and do your best!

Chapter 8

The Deceptions of Wealth

Wealth, like sex, drugs and fame, has an unusually strong effect on people. Everyone knows sex, drugs and fame will seriously influence us, but for some reason, we resist the idea that wealth will affect us. We don't want to believe we could be "that person," who is changed by wealth.

Ironically, failing to recognize wealth's power over us will only amplify its effect. Its effects can be subtle and change us slowly over long periods of time. Jesus makes this point abundantly clear in the Parable of the Sower.

> *Still others, like seed sown among thorns, hear the word; but the worries of this life, the deceitfulness of wealth and the desires for other things come in and choke the word, making it unfruitful.* (Mark 4:18-19)

There's a lot to say about the dangers of wealth, some of which are covered elsewhere in this book. But this chapter is specifically devoted to the ways in which wealth deceives us. Jesus portrays mammon as a dangerous con man, whose goal is to kill the gospel and make your life unfruitful.

WEALTH MAKES YOU THINK YOU'RE SMARTER THAN YOU ACTUALLY ARE

> *The rich are wise in their own eyes;*
> *one who is poor and discerning sees how deluded they are.* (Proverbs 28:11)

This one is tricky, because making wise decisions often leads to wealth. So if we've made a lot of money, we must have a lot of wisdom, right? Isn't the proof in the pudding? However, that is a classic logical fallacy. We ascribe a cause to an effect without properly accounting for other variables. Logically speaking, you can't assume wisdom simply because of wealth, even if it was earned.

In psychological terms, this phenomenon might be referred to as a type of attribution bias called the self-serving bias.[23] It refers to people's tendency to attribute their successes to internal factors but attribute their failures to external factors. Psychologists consider this to be an ego protection mechanism. Christians might call this pride.

> *Better a poor but wise youth than an old but foolish king*
> *who no longer knows how to heed a warning.*
> *(Ecclesiastes 4:13)*

The problem with thinking we're wiser than we are is that it tends to close us off to learning. After all, why listen to others when you have all the answers? That kind of mentality chokes off personal growth and is bad for business!

> *Joyful is the person who finds wisdom,*
> *   the one who gains understanding.*
> *For wisdom is more profitable than silver,*
> *   and her wages are better than gold.*
> *(Proverbs 3:13-14 NLT)*

> *Choose my instruction rather than silver,*
> *   and knowledge rather than pure gold.*
> *For wisdom is far more valuable than rubies.*
> *   Nothing you desire can compare with it.*
> *(Proverbs 8:10-11 NLT)*

> *How much better to get wisdom than gold,*
> *   and good judgment than silver!*
> *(Proverbs 16:16 NLT)*

These passages place wisdom above riches; so much so that it juxtaposes them to make them seem mutually incompatible. Here, the Bible just seems downright un-American! Should we really pursue wisdom instead of money? Is wisdom really better than wealth? Absolutely.

If you really take these Scriptures to heart, it could radically change your long-term goals and plans. Instead of a beefy 401(k), you might be seeking spiritual learning experiences. This kind of thinking could also affect your short-term goals as well. Instead of trying to get ahead at work or in your business, you might focus on the quality of your work and relationships.

The effect that riches has upon us is not something to be taken lightly. Whether you have a thousand or a million in the bank, you should humble yourself before God and man, and fight to keep perspective. Always be looking for opportunities to learn and take captive arrogant thoughts (2 Corinthians 10:5).

WEALTH GIVES YOU THE FALSE IMPRESSION THAT YOU'RE PHYSICALLY SECURE

The rich think of their wealth as a strong defense;
they imagine it to be a high wall of safety.
(Proverbs 18:11 NLT)

Wealth can do a lot, almost anything it seems (Ecclesiastes 10:19b *"money is the answer for everything"*). But Solomon warns us that it has its limitations. Jesus gives us a similar warning in the Parable of the Rich Fool (Luke 12:13-21). In that parable, a rich man was set to die on the very night he decided to build bigger barns to store his wealth.

Wisdom is a shelter
as money is a shelter,
but the advantage of knowledge is this:
Wisdom preserves those who have it.
(Ecclesiastes 7:12)

This passage reminds me of the story of David, Nabal, and Abigail in 1 Samuel 25. Nabal was very wealthy but refused to provide food for David and his men, though David had previously benefitted Nabal. David was enraged and decided to kill Nabal and the men in his household. Abigail, Nabal's wife, wisely rushed out to appease David. Nabal, on the other hand, ended up dying of heart failure after hearing about what almost happened.

Is God trying to scare us into generosity? Perhaps, but I think the larger message is that our wealth does not protect our life. It can make us comfortable and powerful, but when it is our time to go, nothing can stop it (Ecclesiastes 8:8). Wealth or no wealth, we must honor God and keep in perspective who has the real power over our lives.

The story of King Nebuchadnezzar in Daniel sums this up well. Daniel's prophecy describes Nebuchadnezzar's kingdom (the Babylonian empire) as the *"head of gold"* over the later Medo-Persian, Greek, and Roman empires. The king was possibly the richest man to ever live. Despite having the great prophet Daniel as his chief advisor, the king was consumed by wealth, greed and power.

> *"Therefore, Your Majesty, be pleased to accept my advice: Renounce your sins by doing what is right, and your wickedness by being kind to the oppressed. It may be that then your prosperity will continue."* (Daniel 4:27)

King Nebuchadnezzar ignored the advice. Daniel prophesied that the king would go insane for a period of time, then come to his senses. The king *"was driven away from people and ate grass like the ox"* until he praised God (v. 33). The king told this story to his entire kingdom ending with these words:

> *"Now I, Nebuchadnezzar, praise and exalt and glorify the King of heaven, because everything he does is right and all his ways are just. And those who walk in pride he is able to humble."* (Daniel 4:37)

Wealth has its place, but it is only important to a point. Our time on the earth is determined by God and no amount of wealth can change that. We only control what we do with the time and wealth that we have.

WEALTH PROMISES US HAPPINESS, BUT NEVER DELIVERS

Now that you have wealth, you've crossed over into the financial promised land. Or have you?

From the days of Adam, God cursed man with the burden of painful toil in order to produce food (Genesis 3:17). Throughout most of human history, it was necessary to store up provisions in order to survive. Wealth building is a natural human instinct that gives us security, comfort, pleasure and a profound sense of accomplishment. It's literally in our DNA.

Even children exhibit instinctive hoarding at a very early age. If you don't know what I'm talking about, just watch toddlers playing together with toys. God gave us this basic survival instinct, but as adults we take it to illogical extremes.

> *I have seen a grievous evil under the sun:*
> *wealth hoarded to the harm of its owners.*
> (Ecclesiastes 5:13)

Because of the advance of technology, we live in an age where many of us have far more than we need. This plenty, ironically, puts us in a dangerous position emotionally and spiritually. Even a scientific study has proven that wealth beyond a certain point does not make us happy.[24]

> *I have a lot of friends who have a lot more possessions.*
> *But in some cases, I feel the possessions possess them, rather than the other way around.* —Warren Buffett

As always, the Bible is way ahead of man's wisdom. Jesus warns us of the futility and dangers of wealth: *"Watch out! Be on your guard against all kinds of greed; life does not consist in an abundance of possessions."* (Luke 12:15). The Apostle Paul famously advised his protégé Timothy that ... *"the love of money is a root of all kinds of evil. Some people, eager for money, have wandered from the faith and pierced themselves with many griefs."* (1 Timothy 6:10).

Why can't we reach a certain point in building wealth and then be satisfied? It would seem logical that when our basic needs are met, we could then focus on higher pursuits than accumulating wealth. Psychologists would explain this illogical human behavior by saying that our expectations and desires rise to meet any standard of living we achieve. This human phenomenon is often referred to as the "hedonic treadmill."

Christian or not, all of us in the modern world are on the hedonic treadmill to some degree. Our time, energy and joy are spent in a never-ending mad dash. Often, achieving material success makes us more depressed, because when happiness doesn't come with it, we lose all hope of ever feeling fulfilled. Of course, we are looking for happiness in the wrong place.

Lottery winners are perhaps the most extreme experiment in showing that wealth does not produce happiness. I recently read about a British teen who won the Euromillions lottery when she was 17.[25] She spends some of her time on talk shows complaining about her unhappiness. People are disgusted by her complaining, but the public simultaneously finds her unhappiness fascinating.

Ever since I started writing this book, I looked for interesting examples of unhappy lottery winners in the news. I wanted to make a strong point, but then, I started seeing the stories everywhere. It seemed passé to recount one of these all too common stories. These stories really aren't newsworthy, because the results are predictable.

We know that almost every lottery winner ends up unhappy and broke, but then why do we keep buying tickets? Why does the Mega Millions sign with the jackpot number entice us? It's because we think it will be different for us. God knows, I'd like to try out winning 789 million dollars. It could be different for me, right?

> *But godliness with contentment is great gain. For we brought nothing into the world, and we can take nothing out of it. But if we have food and clothing, we will be content with that.* (1 Timothy 6:6-8)

We don't need to win the lottery to be happy. We don't need to reach that next financial milestone to be content. God offers us godliness and contentment free of charge. We just need to let go of the idea that wealth makes us happy.

WEALTH MAKES US BELIEVE WE DON'T NEED GOD

> *"To the angel of the church in Laodicea write:*
> *...You say, 'I am rich; I have everything I want. I don't need a thing!' And you don't realize that you are wretched and miserable and poor and blind and naked.*
> (Revelation 3:14a, 17)

Laodicea was wealthy city, renowned for its banking services and products, including eye salve medication. Jesus used specific facts about the city to deliver a compelling warning against that church's worldly character. What warning would Jesus deliver to the Christians in your city? What clever play on words would he use?

I don't think it's any coincidence that the Laodicean church felt it didn't "need a thing." Author Neil Hood says: "The central issue here is this: if you have faith in yourself, who needs faith in the Lord? This is a particular challenge in an age that values individualism, independence, and self-development. ... It is probably fair to say that, in our diverse and shrinking world, consumerism is the religion of the twenty-first century. It's the part of the globalization process that reaches into most corners of the world."[26]

> **Money is essentially a claim to future help from other people. After a lifetime of use, it can become very easy to put our trust in money (or man).**

Take a step back and think about what modern money really is. Does it have intrinsic value? No, it's just pieces of paper-like cloth or digits in a computer! However, mankind accepts it as credit for future goods and services. You store money, because you expect to be able to later redeem it for goods and services. When you are in debt, you expect to later pay it with goods and services.

Money is essentially a claim to future help from other people. After a lifetime of use, it can become very easy to put our trust in money (or man). Of course, one of the recurring themes in the Bible is trusting in God and not man. Trusting in man leads to ruin. It is indeed ironic that the United States' official motto, "In God We Trust," is emblazoned on its currency.

How about us? What do we need from God? I also don't think it's a coincidence that many first-world churches in today's day and age are spiritually lethargic. I am as guilty as anyone of being comfortably numb in my first-world trappings. We need to push ourselves and heed the warning given to the Israelites who were entering the Promised Land.

> *When you have eaten and are satisfied, praise the LORD your God for the good land he has given you. Be careful that you do not forget the LORD your God, failing to observe his commands, his laws and his decrees that I am giving you this day. Otherwise, when you eat and are satisfied, when you build fine houses and settle down, and when your herds and flocks grow large and your silver and gold increase and all you have is multiplied, then your heart will become proud and you will forget the LORD your God, who brought you out of Egypt, out of the land of slavery. He led you through the vast and dreadful wilderness, that thirsty*

> *and waterless land, with its venomous snakes and scorpions. He brought you water out of hard rock. He gave you manna to eat in the wilderness, something your ancestors had never known, to humble and test you so that in the end it might go well with you. You may say to yourself, "My power and the strength of my hands have produced this wealth for me." But remember the LORD your God, for it is he who gives you the ability to produce wealth, and so confirms his covenant, which he swore to your ancestors, as it is today.*
>
> *If you ever forget the LORD your God and follow other gods and worship and bow down to them, I testify against you today that you will surely be destroyed. Like the nations the Lord destroyed before you, so you will be destroyed for not obeying the LORD your God.*
> (Deuteronomy 8:10-20 see also Hosea 13:6)

Although wealth is morally neutral, it is spiritual nitroglycerin. We might try to use the explosive to destroy our enemies, but it is just as likely to blow us up! Our sinful human nature leads us to take credit for our wealth, become arrogant, and blow up our relationship with God. We may have prayed to land that job or to start that business, but we forget about all that when the money starts coming in.

The truth is that we all need God, all of the time. We need him for our joy, fulfillment, purpose, prosperity and future well-being. The idea that we are self-sufficient is, at best, a fleeting illusion that will leave us empty. At worst, it is a vicious lie that will rob us of our salvation.

> *For of this you can be sure: No immoral, impure or greedy person—such a person is an idolater—has any inheritance in the kingdom of Christ and of God.* (Ephesians 5:5)

This is one of the passages that really scares me, because I am all three: immoral, impure and greedy. I'm more comfortable with the passages that condemn outward sins like adultery, because I can know whether or not I'm messing up. In this passage, the standard is much more subjective.

Rather than fearfully ignoring a Scripture like this, I think we need to humbly listen and see how it can change our lives. I suppose the question you have to ask yourself is: "in my heart and in the way

I live my life, am I an immoral, impure and greedy person?" Since we all are, to some degree, perhaps the better question is: "am I willing to actively work on being more moral, pure and generous?" It's critical to guard our hearts and always be striving for spiritual growth.

In the end, even the wise King Solomon let his heart drift away from God.

> As Solomon grew old, his wives turned his heart after other gods, and his heart was not fully devoted to the LORD his God, as the heart of David his father had been. He followed Ashtoreth the goddess of the Sidonians, and Molek the detestable god of the Ammonites. So Solomon did evil in the eyes of the LORD; he did not follow the Lord completely, as David his father had done. (1 Kings 11:4-6)

Why would a King who was so rewarded by God turn from him? Why worship other gods, when it was Yahweh who gave him wisdom, wealth and the kingship? Yes, he married many women who worshipped other gods, but I believe the underlying arrogance and ingratitude came from his wealth. Solomon did great things with his wealth; but in the end, his wealth led him away from God.

Solomon did great things with his wealth; but in the end, his wealth led him away from God.

Solomon went against many of God's regulations for kingship, which included: not acquiring Egyptian horses, taking many wives, and accumulating large amounts of money (Deuteronomy 17:14-20). Instead of gratitude and a focus on God, Solomon chose excess. Rather than condemning Solomon as an unusually ungrateful heretic, I think his end is a sobering warning to us all of the dangers of wealth and arrogance.

Like Solomon, God has given you wealth. Will you be choked by it? Will you look to it for happiness? Will you let it lead you away from God? Or will you see the truth and overcome the deceptions of wealth?

Chapter 9

Riches and Righteousness

What is the relationship between riches and righteousness? Do they come as a package or are they diametrically opposed to each other? There are many Old Testament examples of where God generously blessed the righteous with wealth. Rather than providing those types of narratives, the New Testament supplies warning after warning about the dangers of wealth.

Clearly, there were wealthy disciples (1 Timothy 6:17-19 and Romans 12:6-8). However, it was not an honor to be rich (James 1:10) and Jesus did say that *"it is hard for someone who is rich to enter the kingdom of heaven."* (Matthew 19:23b). This subject can be a little confusing, because there are a number of different issues to consider. So, let's take this on, one issue at a time.

DID I BECOME WEALTHY BECAUSE I HAVE BEEN RIGHTEOUS?

When you look around at others' financial situations compared to your own, what do you see? If you aren't too busy looking at the Joneses, you might see that you have more than most. Remember, when I say wealthy, I don't mean only those with a million plus dollars. I'm talking about anyone who has no bad debt and money to invest. If that's you, *you are wealthy* and in a better position than most!

Did you become wealthy because you were righteous? Were you more righteous than those with less than you? Maybe. Maybe not. Some righteous behaviors produce wealth. Some righteous behaviors reduce your wealth. Some unrighteous behaviors produce wealth. Some unrighteous behaviors reduce wealth.

If you have self-control and don't buy that fancy latte this morning, you are $5 wealthier. If you work hard and earn more at work, that also makes you wealthier. If you consider these righteous behaviors, then perhaps righteousness does contribute to wealth creation. On the other hand, spending your time doing ministry work and giving to the poor depletes your finances. So, from a purely causal perspective, it's really a mixed bag.

Then there's the matter of your starting point. In a race, is it fair if some people start ahead of others? In a game, is it fair if the playing field is tilted in one team's direction? Of course not, but the "game" of life isn't fair at all! Many things are beyond a person's control like how wealthy your family is, where you grow up, how smart you are and even simple luck.

> *I have seen something else under the sun:*
>
> *The race is not to the swift*
> *or the battle to the strong,*
> *nor does food come to the wise*
> *or wealth to the brilliant*
> *or favor to the learned;*
> *but time and chance happen to them all.* (Ecclesiastes 9:11)

This reminds me of a saying an old colleague told me about wealthy business people: "Some people are good, some people are lucky." The first few times I heard that saying I would chuckle, because it was a nice insight into why some are financially successful. But now I know the real meaning of the saying is: stop trying to figure out which is which—it doesn't matter.

> *There is something else meaningless that occurs on earth: the righteous who get what the wicked deserve, and the wicked who get what the righteous deserve. This too, I say, is meaningless.* (Ecclesiastes 8:14)

So, I don't think you can ever attribute your wealth to your righteousness. We need to remind ourselves of this to avoid becoming self-righteous. By the same token, we shouldn't attribute someone else's wealth to their righteousness. Don't *"be overawed when others grow rich."* (Psalm 49:16).

GOD USES WEALTH TO ACCOMPLISH HIS PURPOSES

Wait a minute! But doesn't God determine how wealthy we are? Look at this Scripture:

> *The LORD sends poverty and wealth;*
> *he humbles and he exalts.* (1 Samuel 2:7)

If God sends poverty and wealth, then we're not really in control of how wealthy we are, right? This type of thinking leads into a philosophical debate between predeterminism and free will, which I won't attempt to address. Whatever you believe about how exactly God accomplishes his will in this universe, a believer in Scripture cannot ignore the fact that God directly intervenes in people's lives using poverty and wealth.

> So, I don't think you can ever attribute your wealth to your righteousness. We need to remind ourselves of this to avoid becoming self-righteous.

Truly, O God of Israel, our Savior,
you work in mysterious ways. (Isaiah 45:15 NLT)

Have you ever felt God using your financial ups and downs to challenge your spiritual condition? Perhaps you've noticed God using financial opportunities or hardships to guide some of your major life decisions? Rather than a barometer of righteousness, God uses wealth to accomplish his purposes on earth and in your life.

WEALTH HAS NO DISCERNABLE RELATIONSHIP TO RIGHTEOUSNESS

Perhaps the most extreme example of righteousness not aligning with fortunes is found in the book of Job. At first, righteous Job is given wealth and honor by God. After God brags about him, Satan challenges God on whether Job is righteous only because of God's blessings. God allows Satan to test him with tremendous loss and illness. Nearly the entire book grapples with the issue of whether our temporary situation matches with our righteousness. The answer is a resounding no!

God ends up blessing Job with more than he had before his trials. Job's life was a storybook drama with a storybook ending. By contrast, Jesus grew up middle class and lived very modestly (by choice) during his ministry years. He was not honored with wealth until his ascension into heaven. There's no one-size-fits-all way that righteous people's lives play out.

There is, however, an underlying theme that the righteous will eventually be rewarded. Of course, God's rewards are not just financial. Whatever the rewards God has for us, it is unknown when and how those rewards will come. Just because we don't see an immediate reward in our lives, we cannot give up trying to please God. God knows our efforts and sees our hearts.

> *And without faith it is impossible to please God, because anyone who comes to him must believe that he exists and that he rewards those who earnestly seek him.* (Hebrews 11:6)

In summary, we cannot measure our lives, much less our righteousness, in dollars and cents. We can never know our reward from God until the very end. A person's wealth is no indicator of their spiritual status. It just is what it is. And what it means, we do not know.

IS THE GOSPEL ALSO A GOSPEL OF PROSPERITY?

The prosperity gospel (a.k.a. the health and wealth gospel) "is a religious belief among some Christians, who hold that financial blessing and physical well-being are always the will of God for them, and that faith, positive speech, and donations to religious causes will increase one's material wealth."[27] While most Christians don't believe this type of extreme teaching, we may subscribe to a version of it, which I call "prosperity gospel lite."

Prosperity gospel lite is the idea that God materially rewards you for your faith or service. We tend to read Scriptures like this with an egocentric view:

> *"...For I know the plans I have for you,"* declares the LORD, *"plans to prosper you and not to harm you, plans to give you hope and a future.* (Jeremiah 29:11)

Many latch onto the hopeful language but fail to read the context of this promise. We individualize the word *"you"* and read this to mean God has a prosperous future for everyone who follows him.[28] The *"you"* in the passage corporately refers to Israel. Western eyes tend to misread Scriptures that refer to groups of people and apply them to individuals.

Even though God had mercy and good plans for his people, they were long-term plans. Israel suffered through death, slavery and subjugation for two generations following the prophecy of Jeremiah. God eventually re-established the nation of Israel through Persian kings and leaders like Ezra and Nehemiah. Did God love the people in the later generations more than those in the earlier ones? Of course not.

You may think, as I have, that if God has a good plan for his people collectively, then by extension, he has a good plan for me. The problem is that our idea of a good plan typically includes material prosperity and worldly success. God's plan for your life may or may not have those things in it. Don't get me wrong, I do believe that God is working in our lives and wants to give us good things. However, he does not prioritize our individual prosperity over our individual spiritual growth or his larger purposes on earth.

If anyone teaches otherwise and does not agree to the sound instruction of our Lord Jesus Christ and to godly teaching, they are conceited and understand nothing. They have an unhealthy interest in controversies and quarrels about words that result in envy, strife, malicious talk, evil suspicions and constant friction between people of corrupt mind, who have been robbed of the truth and who think that godliness is a means to financial gain. (1 Timothy 6:3-5)

Jesus doesn't promise his followers material prosperity or worldly success. But because many of us have the prosperity gospel lite deep in our psyche, we can feel God is against us or doesn't love us when things don't go just right in our life. It can warp our relationship with God and cause us to misunderstand what God is doing in our lives. These misunderstandings can lead to bitterness and great spiritual harm.

> **A person's wealth is no indicator of their spiritual status. It just is what it is. And what it means, we do not know.**

This thinking also creeps into our mindset about giving. You may have heard it said that, "you can't out give God." This saying implies that God will quickly repay you for your contribution and give you even more. While God does reward us, we shouldn't expect God to give us material prosperity right back. Where then would our reward in heaven be? This kind of thinking is unsound and ungodly.

Prosperity gospel lite subtly feeds into the larger idea that your financial well-being is a measure of your righteousness. The thinking might go like this: if God materially rewards faithfulness and sacrifice, then you must be unrighteous if things aren't going well for you financially. We need to reject these subtle beliefs and always have an open mind to what God is doing in our lives.

HOW DOES MODERN CULTURE AFFECT MY VIEWPOINT ABOUT WEALTH?

*One person pretends to be rich, yet has nothing;
another pretends to be poor, yet has great wealth.*
(Proverbs 13:7)

Why does the millionaire next door drive a 15-year-old car and the broke guy drive an $80,000 sports car? Perception. We care what people think. What is your gut reaction to the wealthy? We've already stated that wealth is neutral, and logic would allow us to have no other conclusion. But we humans aren't always logical beings, and we are especially blind to our cultural and emotional biases.

In the ancient world, including ancient Judea, most people generally assumed the rich were corrupt or exploiting the poor.[29] Some cultures still maintain this bias today. This assumption is based on the view that wealth is a limited resource. In other words, if you have wealth, then someone else doesn't. And there are many someones who are needier than you.

> Our culture values hard work, ingenuity, skill, winning and bold risk-taking. These are some of our culture's greatest virtues. Although not necessarily biblical, we might treat them as such.

The Bible, having been written with an Eastern cultural mindset, tends to reflect this viewpoint. In contrast, most of the world today views wealth as unlimited resource. This belief makes the rich creators of wealth, rather than hoarders. I can see some truth in both underlying viewpoints.

Generally speaking, first-world citizens today celebrate wealth and the wealthy. We diligently study books on how they made their wealth, in the hopes we might gain insights. We want to know all about their personal lives through the media. Many movies and small-screen series involve the lives of the wealthy. Wealth is glamorous and interesting.

Our culture values hard work, ingenuity, skill, winning and bold risk-taking. These are some of our culture's greatest virtues. Although not necessarily biblical, we might treat them as such. We were raised with those values and teach them to our children, because we believe it is important for them to thrive in our respective societies. Perhaps rightly so, but it is easy to confuse our values with God's values.

The ascent of the Western world appears to prove that Western values are right. How can the values that have brought so much power and success be contradicted? We believe the accumulation of wealth is the result of putting these virtues into practice. So, it follows that those who are wealthy must be righteous. Although this is a logical fallacy, we deep down inside tend to believe it is generally true.

Although we may envy those wealthier than ourselves, we tend to look up to them and give them automatic respect. We can give their opinions more weight, even when it comes to spiritual matters. As in all matters, we should resist our biases and base our judgments on the Scriptures and sound evidence.

CAN I BE A RICH CHRISTIAN?

As previously stated, the answer is yes. But then how can this Scripture be explained:

> *As Jesus started on his way, a man ran up to him and fell on his knees before him. "Good teacher," he asked, "what must I do to inherit eternal life?"*
>
> *"Why do you call me good?" Jesus answered. "No one is good—except God alone. You know the commandments: 'You shall not murder, you shall not commit adultery, you shall not steal, you shall not give false testimony, you shall not defraud, honor your father and mother.'"*
>
> *"Teacher," he declared, "all these I have kept since I was a boy."*
>
> *Jesus looked at him and loved him. "One thing you lack," he said. "Go, sell everything you have and give to the poor, and you will have treasure in heaven. Then come, follow me."*
>
> *At this the man's face fell. He went away sad, because he had great wealth.*
>
> *Jesus looked around and said to his disciples, "How hard it is for the rich to enter the kingdom of God!"*
>
> *The disciples were amazed at his words. But Jesus said again, "Children, how hard it is to enter the kingdom of God! It is easier for a camel to go through the eye of a needle than for someone who is rich to enter the kingdom of God."*
>
> *The disciples were even more amazed, and said to each other, "Who then can be saved?"*
>
> *Jesus looked at them and said, "With man this is impossible, but not with God; all things are possible with God."*

Then Peter spoke up, *"We have left everything to follow you!"*

"Truly I tell you," Jesus replied, *"no one who has left home or brothers or sisters or mother or father or children or fields for me and the gospel will fail to receive a hundred times as much in this present age: homes, brothers, sisters, mothers, children and fields—along with persecutions—and in the age to come eternal life. But many who are first will be last, and the last first."* (Mark 10:17-31 parallel accounts are in Luke 18:18-30 and Matthew 19:1-30)

After reading this, you might conclude that you cannot be rich and be saved. Jesus commanded the young man to *"sell everything you have and give to the poor."* However, Jesus did not command anyone else to sell everything they have—not even the apostles. Why did Jesus give such a difficult command to this young man?

Perhaps it was because the young man was especially reliant on his wealth and it kept him from truly giving his heart to God. Perhaps it was to make a point. Here is an especially good commentary on the meaning of the Scripture:

> *There are several different schools of thought on what Jesus was referring to in saying it was easier for a camel to go through the eye of a needle than for a rich man to gain eternal life (Matthew 19:24; Mark 10:25; Luke 18:25). The Persians expressed the concept of the impossible by saying it would be easier to put an elephant through the eye of a needle. The camel was a Jewish adaptation (the largest animal in Israel was a camel).*
>
> *Some theorize that the needle Jesus was speaking of was the Needle Gate, supposedly a low and narrow after-hours entrance found in the wall surrounding Jerusalem. It was purposely small for security reasons, and a camel could only go through it by stripping off any saddles or packs and crawling through on its knees. The problem with this theory is there is no evidence such a gate ever existed. Beyond that, what sane camel driver would go through such contortions when larger gates were easily accessible?*
>
> *Some claim that the word translated "camel" (Greek: kamelos) should actually be "cable" (Greek: kamilos). Then*

the verse would read that it is easier for a cable (or rope) to go through the eye of a needle. To believe this, however, brings up more problems than it solves, casting doubt on the inerrancy and inspiration of Scripture.

The most likely explanation is that Jesus was using hyperbole, a figure of speech that exaggerates for emphasis. Jesus used this technique at other times, referring to a "plank" in one's eye (Matthew 7:3-5) and swallowing a camel (Matthew 23:24).

Jesus' message is clear—it is impossible for anyone to be saved on his own merits. Since wealth was seen as proof of God's approval, it was commonly taught by the rabbis that rich people were blessed by God and were, therefore, the most likely candidates for heaven. Jesus destroyed that notion, and along with it, the idea that anyone can earn eternal life. The disciples had the appropriate response to this startling statement. They were utterly amazed and asked, "Who then can be saved?" in the next verse. If the wealthy among them, which included the super-spiritual Pharisees and scribes, were unworthy of heaven, what hope was there for a poor man?

In contrast to the underlying Eastern view on wealth, we see that the gospel of prosperity also reared its ugly head in ancient Judea. Even the apostles' view of who was righteous was distorted by wealth. We can easily fall prey to believing our own spiritual condition is solid, because our finances are solid (and vice versa). Nothing could be further from the truth.[30]

AM I PREJUDICED IN FAVOR OF THE WEALTHY AND AGAINST THE POOR?

My brothers and sisters, believers in our glorious Lord Jesus Christ must not show favoritism. Suppose a man comes into your meeting wearing a gold ring and fine clothes, and a poor man in filthy old clothes also comes in. If you show special attention to the man wearing fine clothes and say, "Here's a good seat for you," but say to the poor man, "You stand there" or "Sit on the floor by my feet," have you not discriminated among yourselves and become judges with evil thoughts?

> *Listen, my dear brothers and sisters: Has not God chosen those who are poor in the eyes of the world to be rich in faith and to inherit the kingdom he promised those who love him? But you have dishonored the poor. Is it not the rich who are exploiting you? Are they not the ones who are dragging you into court? Are they not the ones who are blaspheming the noble name of him to whom you belong?* (James 2:1-7)

How do we treat the poor in our congregations? Do you give them equal respect with the wealthy or are we biased against them? Although we may not outwardly discriminate against poor people, do we do it in our hearts?

> *Listen, my dear brothers and sisters: Has not God chosen those who are poor in the eyes of the world to be rich in faith and to inherit the kingdom he promised those who love him?* (James 2:5)

James is speaking to Christians who were being oppressed by wealthy Jews. These Jews were using their wealth as a weapon of persecution, but God has a way of leveling out the playing field. The poor are excluded from many things in society, but not from the kingdom of God. Do we act in a way that excludes the poor from the kingdom of God?

AM I ADVOCATING WORKS SALVATION?

Many Scriptures and their accompanying points in this book might lead you to think I am saying you must do works to make it to heaven. Well, I am and that's what I think many of the Scriptures are actually saying to all of us. That is very different than saying those works will earn you passage to heaven. We are saved by grace, but that grace does not give us license to sin (Romans 6:1-4).

God will judge us according to his word, not my book. So, we must decide for ourselves what the Bible is really saying and its implications. As much as I want to believe my salvation is secure no matter what I do, my reading of the Scriptures tells me otherwise. This Scripture comes to mind:

> *Therefore, my dear friends, as you have always obeyed—not only in my presence, but now much more in my*

absence—continue to work out your salvation with fear and trembling, for it is God who works in you to will and to act in order to fulfill his good purpose. (Philippians 2:12-13)

Although this isn't a book about how to be saved *per se*, it covers many areas where the Bible makes clear that salvation hangs in the balance. None of us will be perfect. Not even the best of us will measure up. But, we must keep our lamps burning and stay within his grace.

STRIKING A BALANCE

And I saw that all toil and all achievement spring from one person's envy of another. Fools fold their hands and ruin themselves. Better one handful with tranquility than two handfuls with toil and chasing after the wind. (Ecclesiastes 4:4-6)

According to this passage, the hardworking, achieving person is driven by envy. Older Bible translations read like this: *"I saw that for all toil and every skillful work a man is envied by his neighbor."* (NKJV v5). When you really think about it, both are equally true. I don't think Solomon was trying to condemn being motivated and hard working. Rather, he was trying to highlight the dangers of extremes.

If we don't keep our desire for wealth in check, our greed can drive us to envy. Just look at these psalms and how the psalmist comes to a faithful conclusion.

Better the little that the righteous have
 than the wealth of many wicked;
for the power of the wicked will be broken,
 but the LORD upholds the righteous.

The blameless spend their days under the LORD's care,
 and their inheritance will endure forever.
In times of disaster they will not wither;
 in days of famine they will enjoy plenty. (Psalm 37:16-19)

Surely God is good to Israel,
 to those who are pure in heart.
But as for me, my feet had almost slipped;

> *I had nearly lost my foothold.*
> *For I envied the arrogant*
> *when I saw the prosperity of the wicked. ...*
> *When I tried to understand all this,*
> *it troubled me deeply*
> *till I entered the sanctuary of God;*
> *then I understood their final destiny. ...*
> *But as for me, it is good to be near God.*
> *I have made the Sovereign LORD my refuge;*
> *I will tell of all your deeds.* (Psalm 73:1-3, 16-17, 28)

When we see wealthier people than ourselves who we deem wicked, we're tempted to be bitter at God because we envy them. We think to ourselves, "why be righteous?" We are tempted to abandon our righteousness in order to pursue the path of the people that we see. Some of us quickly go there. Some of us have a higher tolerance for it.

Even when we do things righteously, we can become unrighteous by simply pursuing wealth too much. After a couple of years of hard work at a law firm, my boss approached me about working even harder so that I might become his junior business partner. Even though I was putting in consistent 60-hour weeks, he encouraged me to sacrifice my late evenings and weekends to attend marketing groups and to further familiarize myself with the latest case law trends. My boss subtly goaded me by saying he wanted me to do more, but it was okay if I just wanted to be a "worker bee."[31]

I had the skill and ambition to go further, but my spiritual life and personal life were both suffering. I valued time with my wife and personal time, which had become very minimal. I also valued spending time in church leadership, evangelism, and other activities. Working 60 hours a week didn't leave a lot left. Part of me wanted to go for it, but I just couldn't bring myself to fully commit myself to my work (i.e. consistent 70+ hour weeks). I already worked every Saturday and late most evenings. After I had children, I reached a breaking point in which I decided to flee working as a litigator.

Call me a wimp. You can say that I didn't have what it took. In a sense, that is true. Maybe if the circumstances were different, I might have happily made partner somewhere else. Maybe if the commitment wasn't so extreme or if I didn't have other passions, I might have done it. But it doesn't matter, because you only have one life and experience one set of circumstances in which to make decisions. For me in my circumstance, it just wasn't worth it spiritually or personally.

I tell that story not to say a Christian couldn't go to extremes and survive spiritually, though I believe that person would certainly pay a price. Each to their own! God made us to each have different tolerances for extremes in our lives. We know we are going too far when our righteousness, consciences and faith suffer. The author of this proverb understood the importance of balance:

> *"Two things I ask of you, LORD;*
> *do not refuse me before I die:*
> *Keep falsehood and lies far from me;*
> *give me neither poverty nor riches,*
> *but give me only my daily bread.*
> *Otherwise, I may have too much and disown you*
> *and say, 'Who is the LORD?'*
> *Or I may become poor and steal,*
> *and so dishonor the name of my God.* (Proverbs 30:7-9)

If we are poor, we might need to go to some extremes in order to survive. It takes faith and self-control to avoid being unrighteous in those circumstances. Likewise, the extreme pursuit of wealth leads us away from God. We must achieve a balance that keeps us strong spiritually.

> *[People] have become so indoctrinated with the idea that having money is important, that they no longer question why. They are unaware that perhaps what they are truly seeking is an increase in self-respect, or security, or freedom, or love, or power.*[32]

Some of us can operate at full steam "earning all we can, saving all we can and giving away all we can." (quoting John Wesley).[33] But for some of us, we need to slow down and spend more time with God, church, and family.[34] If you're feeling this way, I encourage you to meditate on these passages:

> *Don't wear yourself out trying to get rich.*
> *Be wise enough to know when to quit.*

(Proverbs 23:4 NLT)

*The earnings of the godly enhance their lives,
   but evil people squander their money on sin.*
(Proverbs 10:16 NLT)

*Better what the eye sees
   than the roving of the appetite.
This too is meaningless,
   a chasing after the wind.* (Ecclesiastes 6:9)

Some of us are just fine and can handle even more work responsibilities, but some us need to back off for the sake of our family and relationship with God. Some of us have damaged consciences and need to add righteousness to our business or work practices. As our life situation changes, we can't be afraid to reevaluate what is right for our lives. At the end of the day, we have to remember that wealth is just the means and not the end.

Chapter 10

Worry & Money

Therefore I tell you, do not worry about your life, what you will eat or drink; or about your body, what you will wear. Is not life more than food, and the body more than clothes? Look at the birds of the air; they do not sow or reap or store away in barns, and yet your heavenly Father feeds them. Are you not much more valuable than they? Can any one of you by worrying add a single hour to your life?
(Matthew 6:25-27)

This chapter is for me and maybe it's for you too. I'm constantly tempted to worry and obsess about money because it's in my nature. Because *"money is the answer for everything,"* it can become the place keeper and focal point for all our worries in life (Ecclesiastes 10:19b).

If your wealth is decreasing, it is of great concern. If your wealth is stagnating, it is very troubling. If your wealth is increasing slowly, it isn't growing fast enough. If your wealth is increasing quickly, you worry about what to do with it. If you are a worrier, you know what I am talking about.

> **Worry is a futile endeavor, making us into something less than God intended.**

Our financial situations are the source of great anxiety, focus, and concern. When you worry, you cannot separate legitimate concern from irrational fear. Worry makes us unhappy, irritable, exhausted and faithless.

Worry is a futile endeavor, making us into something less than God intended. Though we try, worry cannot be put in a box and rationalized away. No spreadsheet, line graph or flush bank statement can free us from what ails us, because it is a spiritual condition.

REASONS TO WORRY?

The world today gives us plenty of reasons to worry. We're inundated with expenses, which are constantly rising. From 1989 to

2017, inflation in America made the same things twice as expensive.[35] Wages have hardly kept up. For many, their purchasing power has eroded over the years.

For many years after the 2008 financial crisis, the financial media has told us that inflation has been very low. You may have even heard that economists were concerned about the low inflation, and that world central banks needed to address the issue through monetary policies like quantitative easing. There may be some egg-headed rationale for more inflation, but I think most people would beg to differ.

Most people's largest expenses are already high and rising very quickly. Unless you are exceptionally wealthy, you've felt the pressure of increased housing, education, healthcare, automobile and food costs. It is of little consolation that flat-screen TVs are getting cheaper.

As of early-2019, housing, including rents, are at all-time highs in most places. A home is no longer just a place to live, but also most people's largest financial investment. Buying and selling your home is a transaction that could very well make you or break you financially. The increased cost of rents has become a stumbling block for those trying to save up for a down payment for a home.

The cost of higher education is astronomical. When you (or your kids) graduate, there may or may not be gainful employment available. Student loans are not dischargeable in bankruptcy. At best, college has become expensive, reducing any potential return on investment. At worst, it has become the entry way into a life-long debtors' prison.

The cost of healthcare has become staggering, with no signs of letting up. Many cannot afford it. For those that can, premiums have become an increasing drain on paychecks. For the seriously ill, dealing with health insurance coverage has become a life and death situation, physically and financially. Reality is slowly setting in: higher education and quality healthcare are becoming luxuries, rather than mainstays.

In the last few decades, globalization has hollowed out the middle class by moving manufacturing and other labor-oriented jobs to developing economies (of course, this dynamic benefitted workers in those places). Now, automation, robotics and artificial intelligence threatens to displace a whole new set of workers, including some white-collar workers. Society is ever more productive, but most do not share in that increase. Perhaps your livelihood is threatened?

Most of us try to address these and other financial worries by making as much money as we can. The perceived need for ever-increasing wealth drains away our joy and generosity. How can we think of others when we have so much to worry about? The financial challenges we all face are very real and must be addressed, but we should not worry or obsess over them.

THE OLD MAN AND HIS HORSE

We naturally get wound up about our ever-changing circumstances and what-ifs. The story of an old man and his horse has something to teach us:

> *In an ancient Chinese village, there lived an old man who was very poor, but had a sleek and beautiful white horse which no one could match. Kings and noblemen offered fabulous sums of money for the horse, but the old man would decline by saying, "This horse is not a horse to me, but rather a good friend and close companion."*
>
> *One morning, it was discovered that the horse was not in the stable. The whole village gathered, and they said, "You are a foolish old man! We all knew that someday such a fine horse would be stolen. You would have been better off if you had sold it when you had the chance. What a horrible mistake you have made! What a misfortune!" But the old man said, "Do not judge what you do not know. Whether it is a misfortune or a blessing none of us know!"*
>
> *The villagers laughed at the old man. They thought he was crazy. After a couple of weeks, the horse returned. He had not been stolen, but merely escaped temporarily into the wild. Not only did he return, but he brought a dozen wild horses back with him, all of which stood alongside him in the stable.*
>
> *This time the townspeople gathered and proclaimed, "Old man, you were right! This was not a misfortune but has indeed proved to be a great blessing." The old man retorted, "As I said before, do not judge what you do not know. Whether it is a misfortune or a blessing none of us know!" The villagers believed the old man was wrong, because many beautiful horses had miraculously come to him*

without effort.

The old man had an only son who started to train the wild horses. But one day while training the horses, he fell from a horse and broke both his legs. The townspeople gathered once again and said, "Again you are proved to be right! This has become a great misfortune! Because your only son has lost the use of his legs, he cannot support you in your old age." The old man again said, "Do not judge what you do not know. Whether it is a misfortune or a blessing none of us know!"

After a few weeks the country went to war and all the young men of the town were forcibly taken for military service. Only the old man's son was left behind, because he was crippled and unable to walk. The whole town was crying and weeping because everyone knew it was a losing battle, and they were certain that most of the young people would never return.

They gathered around the old man and said, "You were right. Your son's injury has proved to be a blessing. Maybe your son is crippled, but he is still alive and with you. Our sons are gone forever." The old man again said, " Do not judge what you do not know. Whether it is a misfortune or a blessing none of us know!" —Lao Tzu (551-479 B.C.)[36]

Understanding that God is control of the big picture helps us keep an even keel.

HOW TO ADDRESS WORRY

There are many ways to address worry, including reading psychology-based self-help books, which I think is fine. Remember that for most people, worry is a spiritual issue, which should be addressed through Scripture.

1) Be grateful for what you have (make a decision to enjoy life today)

I put this first, because I believe that dealing with worry starts with a decision. I often catch myself worrying and have to tell myself to snap out of it. Strangely, we can get comfortable with worry. It can be that bad-influence friend we feel we can't live without. We're not sure we could get anything done without worry driving us.

> *Why, my soul, are you downcast?*
> *Why so disturbed within me?*
> *Put your hope in God,*
> *for I will yet praise him,*
> *my Savior and my God.* (Psalm 42:5)

When we worry, we focus on what we don't have and what we need for the future. When you focus on what you have now, you see all that God has done for you! If you live in the now, you can be happy and think of the needs of others. If you really want to put things into perspective: make a list of your worries and share it with a friend.

2) Prayer and petition (asking God for joy and help)

> *Do not be anxious about anything, but in every situation, by prayer and petition, with thanksgiving, present your requests to God. And the peace of God, which transcends all understanding, will guard your hearts and your minds in Christ Jesus.* (Philippians 4:6-7)

Really inseparable from gratitude, is taking your worries to God in prayer. You can tell God every single anxiety you have in detail! He won't mind! Sometimes, we don't really know what is bothering us and need some advice. In that case, we need to talk it out with a trusted friend, so that we can better identify our true anxieties and then go to God in prayer.

Sometimes, we get stuck or need to get out of a jam. Pray, pray, pray. There was a point in my life where I was very stressed, dreaded my work, and was without family support near me. It was a dark time in my life.

I needed a new job and a new place to live closer to family support. I prayed earnestly in anguish for a new job opportunity, which God eventually provided. I promised God I would tell everyone about it when he gave me relief. Done! God knows when we really need something, and he readily answers those prayers. What do you need to pray about?

3) Enjoy what you have

> *This is what I have observed to be good: that it is appropriate for a person to eat, to drink and to find satisfaction*

in their toilsome labor under the sun during the few days of life God has given them—for this is their lot. Moreover, when God gives someone wealth and possessions, and the ability to enjoy them, to accept their lot and be happy in their toil—this is a gift of God. They seldom reflect on the days of their life, because God keeps them occupied with gladness of heart. (Ecclesiastes 5:18-20)

What good is wealth if we cannot enjoy it? We should ask God for his gift of enjoyment! We should make sure to take time to enjoy what our wealth can provide. Sometimes it's hard to appropriately enjoy leisure when we are worried. If so, go back to steps 1 and 2. Rinse and repeat!

4) Understand that the Provider provides

Abraham looked up and there in a thicket he saw a ram caught by its horns. He went over and took the ram and sacrificed it as a burnt offering instead of his son. So Abraham called that place The LORD Will Provide. And to this day it is said, "On the mountain of the LORD it will be provided." (Genesis 22:13-14)

God is the great provider (*Jehovah Jireh*)! He made the earth, plants, animals, minerals, and all of us. Providing is in the very nature of God (Philippians 4:19, Psalms 37:25, Matthew 6:31). He is looking for opportunities to provide for us that will build our faith.

5) Reducing risk and turmoil

Better to have little, with fear for the LORD,
than to have great treasure and inner turmoil.
(Proverbs 15:16 NLT)

The sleep of a laborer is sweet,
whether they eat little or much,
but as for the rich, their abundance permits them no sleep. (Ecclesiastes 5:12)

Some of us just have too much risk in our lives—the kind that keeps us up at night. Some of us have too much *"abundance"* to manage. We may need to sell those risky positions or simplify our affairs for our peace of mind.

6) Get some physical exercise

Many of us, myself included, don't get enough physical exercise. God made us to move and sweat. Play sports; go jogging; ride a bike; or hit the gym. Whatever works for you! We are healthier and our mood improves with every calorie burned.

7) Focus on others

But seek first his kingdom and his righteousness, and all these things will be given to you as well. (Matthew 6:33)

Sometimes, we get into a funk, because we just think about ourselves too much. Yes, that includes our responsibilities and liabilities. When our minds are focused on others, we can find joy and contentment.

SUMMARY OF SECTION II

God and money both seek to be our king. We can't take money out of our life, but we can bend it to God's will. God tasks us with investing it and using it for his purposes, which partly includes using it for our enjoyment. However, it is deceptive and dangerous to our souls. It is a tool to meet our needs but can also cause great worry and unhappiness.

After this biblical look at money, how has it affected your mindset? If you are overwhelmed or discouraged, please look to God for the strength to overcome. If you are inspired, I urge you to write down your new vision and how you see your life changing for the better. For many of you, I suspect, true inspiration will only come after taking a leap of faith by putting what you have learned into practice.

Section III:
FINANCIAL INVESTMENTS

Be sure you know the condition of your flocks,
give careful attention to your herds;
for riches do not endure forever,
and a crown is not secure for all generations.
(Proverbs 27:23-24)

Wealth requires your careful attention, at least if you want to keep it. In Solomon's time, wealth was often measured by the size of a person's herds. Now, we have numerous ways to invest and hold wealth. Finding the right investments can be a daunting task.

Whether you are a newbie or a seasoned investor, you have to consider the ramifications of your investment decisions. Each type of financial investment comes with its own unique set of pros and cons, some of which can have serious impacts on your life.

When it comes to your own money, everybody has a Ph.D.
–Jim Rickards[37]

Most of my financial success has come from following sound biblical principles, whether consciously or not. I have carefully observed investment trends and the ebb and flow of the economy. I've noticed that larger economic forces, which are outside of the control and understanding of most people, often end up determining their financial fortunes. In this insecure world, we have every reason to turn to the Bible for answers.

Alright, so are we ready to invest? Here's your first test! Can you tell by looking at this chart if it would be a good time to buy this stock?

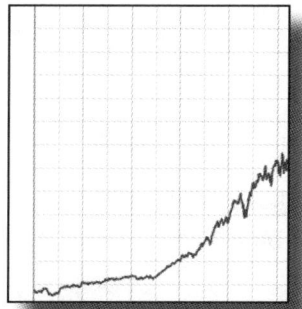

It looks like it's doing great! Would you purchase some? Yes? No? Well, what if later the same stock behaved like this?

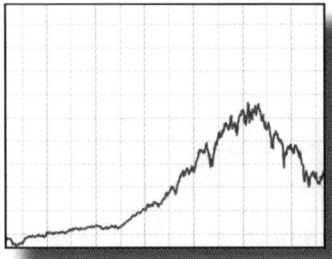

Wow, it took a turn for the worse! Maybe now would be a good time to buy? Maybe it's a good time to sell? Take a look at what happens next.

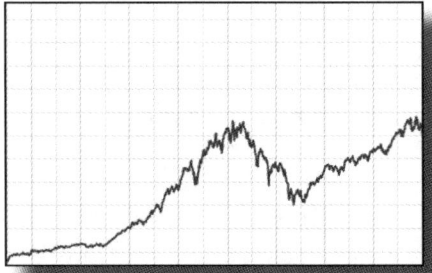

Interesting. If you didn't, you should have bought some! Hindsight is 20/20, but how about now? Let's see what happens next.

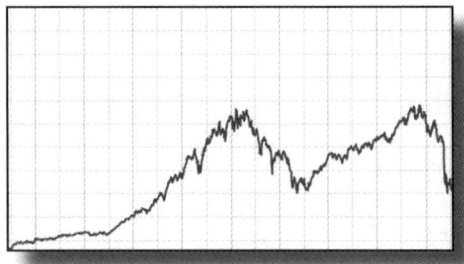

Whoa, I hope your seatbelt is fastened! Should you sell it all before it goes down more? Or is this a good time to buy? Let's see.

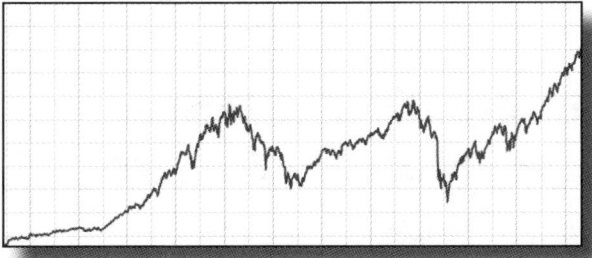

Well hey, what do you know: this is the S&P 500 index from 1990 to 2014! Where do you think it went from that point? Down? No, it kept going up 900 more points to over 2900 (see below)!

This is the S&P 500 index as of May 2019.[38] From where it is today, where will it go? The answer is: no one knows! I hope that's the conclusion you reached too.

Chapter 11

Diversification & Other Biblical Financial Advice

DIVERSIFICATION IS BOTH BIBLICAL AND A WELL-ACCEPTED FINANCIAL STRATEGY

The key to preparing for the unknown future is diversification.

> *Diversification is a risk management technique that mixes a wide variety of investments within a portfolio. The rationale behind this technique contends that a portfolio of different kinds of investments will, on average, yield higher returns and pose a lower risk than any individual investment found within the portfolio. Diversification strives to smooth out unsystematic risk events in a portfolio so that the positive performance of some investments will neutralize the negative performance of others. Therefore, the benefits of diversification will hold only if the securities in the portfolio are not perfectly correlated.* —Investopedia[39]

Diversification is just a fancy way of saying: "Don't put all your eggs in one basket." It's just plain common sense. But for many of us, when we invest, our common sense goes out the window.

The Talmud, the book of rabbinic opinions, recommends that we place our assets: 1/3 in business, 1/3 in real estate, and to keep 1/3 liquid (i.e. cash/gold).[40] Even Shakespeare comments on diversification in the *Merchant of Venice*: "My ventures are not in one bottom trusted, Nor to one place; nor is my whole estate upon the fortune of this present year: Therefore, my merchandise makes me not sad."[41] Every financial professional who has your best interests in mind will tell you to diversify.

Perhaps the earliest and most powerful diversification advice comes from King Solomon. There was no one more qualified than Solomon to give financial advice. His love life may have been a gigantic mess, but he and his kingdom's financial success were unparalleled in his time. What is more: God made him the wisest man to ever live (1 Kings 3:12-13)! So, we ought to pay close attention:

Ship your grain across the sea;
  after many days you may receive a return.
Invest in seven ventures, yes, in eight;
  you do not know what disaster may come upon the land.[42]

If clouds are full of water,
  they pour rain on the earth.
Whether a tree falls to the south or to the north,
  in the place where it falls, there it will lie.
Whoever watches the wind will not plant;
  whoever looks at the clouds will not reap.

As you do not know the path of the wind,
  or how the body is formed in a mother's womb,
so you cannot understand the work of God,
  the Maker of all things.

Sow your seed in the morning,
  and at evening let your hands not be idle,
for you do not know which will succeed,
  whether this or that,
  or whether both will do equally well. (Ecclesiastes 11:1-6)

If you're inclined to keep all your money in your mattress, Solomon sets you straight in Ecclesiastes 11. In fact, he advises investment in "many ventures." Why? It's a way of preparing for disaster. I read the passage to mean that disaster may strike locally, so you should spread out your investments into other geographic areas (e.g. If a hailstorm destroyed your local crops, you could still have income from investments abroad).[43]

DISASTER PREPARATION IS BIBLICAL AND TIMELY

The term "disaster preparation" may sound extreme. Our modern view of "prepping" is a bunch of crazies preparing for the end of the world as we know it. The truth is that anyone who invests is preparing for something. How we invest is just of matter of what we are preparing for. Solomon advised diversification as a way of preparing for disasters that could affect your wealth. Such disasters could include blight, extreme weather events, famine, social upheaval and war.

If you think about it, disasters are pretty common. You may have experienced one personally. We read about them every day in the media. Financial disasters, historically speaking, are also fairly common. Nations' economies implode. Sometimes their currencies collapse. Vast amounts of wealth are routinely destroyed and change hands in a disorderly manner.

> **The truth is that anyone who invests is preparing for something. How we invest is just of matter of what we are preparing for.**

Recently, Venezuela and Zimbabwe have faced currency collapses. Banks in the U.S. and Europe have been "bailed out" by taxpayers (in which savers and pension funds have largely been punished through ultra-low interest rates). Banks in Cyprus have been "bailed in" by depositors. Bondholders of Puerto Rican debt faced heavy losses, because of Puerto Rico's recent insolvency.

Pensioners in Detroit have also accepted heavy losses. Many other municipalities are in serious trouble. Pensioners within fiscally troubled states like Illinois, California, New Jersey, Massachusetts, and Kentucky are not far behind. Many private pensions like that of General Electric and Sears are also in trouble. A prime example is the New York State Teamsters Conference Pension and Retirement Fund, who recently cut its pension payouts by 30%.

The Pension Benefit Guarantee Corporation is the equivalent of what the Federal Deposit Insurance Corporation (FDIC) is to the banks, but it is woefully underfunded and in financial trouble itself. Although you may not be relying on a pension, it will still affect you because of the cascading effects of coming debt write-downs. Additionally, the associated government entities will be forced to increase taxes and reduce government services. Here's part of a 2014 CNBC Article:

OUTLOOK FOR PENSIONS IS PRETTY AWFUL: BRIDGEWATER
Here's a scary retirement prediction: 85 percent of public pensions could fail in 30 years.

> *That's according to the largest hedge fund firm in the world, Bridgewater Associates, which runs $150 billion for pensions and other institutions like endowments and foundations. Public pensions have just $3 trillion in assets to cover liabilities that will balloon to $10 trillion in future decades, Bridgewater said in a client note last week obtained by USA Today. To make up the difference, the firm said pensions will need to earn about 9 percent per year on their investments. But Bridgewater estimates pension funds are more likely to make 4 percent. If that's true, the vast majority—85 percent—of retirement systems will run out of money because they will continue to pay out more than they take in.*[44]

The viability of Social Security and other benefit programs are also in question:

> *The outlook for the program is pretty grim. The trust fund for Social Security's retirement and disability benefits will stop being fully funded in 2034, as projected last year. If no solution is found, promised benefits will take about a 25 percent cut.*[45]

Medicare's hospital insurance trust fund is projected to suffer a similar fate in 2026.[46] That being said, the United States and much of the Western world has enjoyed unprecedented prosperity since World War II.[47] Almost every asset class has steadily appreciated. It has produced generations of Westerners that have no concept or appreciation for significant financial disasters. The "Great Recession" of 2008 was a wake-up call to be sure, but most people feel that things are back to normal.

As of early-2019, the U.S.'s public debt is well over $22,000,000,000,000 (22 trillion dollars).[49] As of the same time frame,

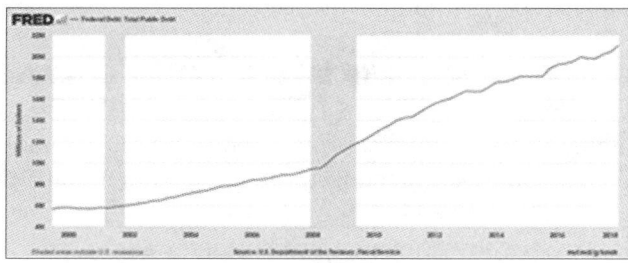

US Total Public Debt from 2000-2018[48]

the U.S.'s total liabilities had exceeded $122,000,000,000,000 (122 trillion dollars). This is what is commonly referred to as "unfunded liabilities." Visualizing a trillion dollars is very difficult for the human mind.[50]

"Here's an astronomical analogy about today's debt: If you stack up 14.3 trillion-dollar bills, the pile would stretch to the moon and back twice."[51] Just 7 years later, the U.S. debt has made another round trip to the moon! Each U.S. citizen owes just over $64,000 in federal government debt alone. Do you think this system is sustainable and that things will continue business as usual? In my opinion, it is only a matter of time before something goes terribly wrong in the U.S. and world financial systems.

> We can sit around wishing we timed the stock market and sold at the top (or bought at the bottom). But real investing doesn't work that way.

That being said, I don't think the world economy will crash this week, this month, or this year (2019). Could it? Sure. Anything is possible. It's more likely to take many years or even decades for the full consequences of the debt to come due. In my opinion, it is like a 50-year-old man who drinks, smokes, and eats way too much fast food. How long will he live and how will he die? Who knows exactly, but the prognosis is bad.

PERSONAL INVESTING DISASTERS

Of course, disasters don't have to be massive or widespread to affect your investments. If you invest your entire net worth in oil stocks, then the price of oil drops for an extended period of time, you've just shipwrecked your finances. But if you had merely invested 1% of your investable assets in oil stocks, then you wouldn't lose any sleep.

The same goes for over-investing in real estate, businesses, mutual funds or anything else. Every asset carries risk, even cash. There's only one safe solution: diversification.

THE BASIC RATIONALE BEHIND DIVERSIFICATION & TIMING MARKETS

If done correctly, diversification allows you to liberally invest while simultaneously protecting the bulk of your wealth that you have already accumulated. Rather than keeping all your wealth in ultra-conservative investments, diversification allows you to place small portions of your wealth in riskier, high-return investments (or medium risk, medium return investments). The general idea is that the gains will outweigh the losses from the higher risk investments if spread out correctly. If you sit in cash and low-risk investments only, your wealth just gets eaten away by inflation.

In short time frames, however, diversification doesn't always appear to work. Sometimes it takes years to see the benefits. For instance, if you invested some funds in a falling stock market for one year, you would be better off in cash. But, after 10-15 years, the general trend of the stock market will typically make you more money. Investing in a diversified manner can take great patience. In many cases, you have to be willing to tie up resources for long periods of time in order to get a good return.

Broad diversification can similarly appear to lose you money. Take, for instance, a hypothetical scenario where you split your investments and place only 25% in the stock market. After the first few years, your total portfolio might lag the stock market, because the stock market has been rocketing up during that time frame. You'll feel like you missed out and wished you had all your money in the stock market. Of course, hindsight is always 20/20. But if over the next two years the stock market crashes, you'll be very glad you were broadly diversified.

We can sit around wishing we timed the stock market and sold at the top (or bought at the bottom). But real investing doesn't work that way. Sadly, most people can't resist and jump in near market tops. Those same people often sell near the bottom and destroy their finances in the process. Even those who tend to be good at it cannot consistently predict market tops and bottoms. Sometimes, we get very lucky. Sometimes, we get very unlucky. That's why we need to broadly diversify.

Because we humans have basic needs, we shouldn't take risks that would leave us without food, clothes, shelter, the means to work, access to health care or retirement money. As a practical matter, that list really should also include money to help our children with their future and money to make future investments for yourselves.

The practical and emotional toll of losing large amounts of money should not be underestimated. But if you are protected through diversification and only lose a modest amount of money, you can carry on without too much grief!

DIVERSIFICATION THROUGH NON-CORRELATED ASSETS

There are many different levels of diversification. Take for instance investing in the tech sector. You might buy only Apple stock with your savings. Instead, you could spread your savings over ten different tech companies' stocks to be more diversified. This is a much safer option, because the next iPhone might be a flop. In that case, nine companies might do well, while only one suffers.

So, by investing in ten companies, you minimize any losses that might be attributable to a particular company. It could be said that Apple's performance is not correlated to the other nine tech companies. This would be an example of a very narrow type of diversification.

But what if you put all your money in tech and the whole sector performs poorly? You would be wise to put money into other sectors, such as utility stocks. If utility stock prices tend to be stable when tech stocks do poorly, then tech and utility assets are not correlated. In some cases, you might want stocks that are inversely correlated. This would be an even broader level of diversification.

One author has even advocated that Solomon's "seven ventures" were actually these seven specific asset classes: 1) large cap stocks, 2) small cap stocks, 3) non-U.S. stocks, 4) commodities and natural resources, 5) Real Estate Investment Trusts (REITs), 6) intermediate bonds, 7) cash.[52] However, it is well known that the use of the number seven in the Bible is often symbolic and typically refers to many or completeness. So, I find the author's breakdown of the "seven ventures" humorous, though I don't disagree with the general thinking. Some of the asset classes listed are not correlated on some level, so the suggested allocation provides some level of diversification.

The scope of non-correlated assets can be expanded pretty far out depending on the type of disaster you are trying to diversify against. Even life and disability insurances are forms of diversification for your family, for a potential loss of income. What about protecting against a full-blown stock market or currency collapse? We will discuss this in later chapters, but the important concept is non-correlation, which is the key to broad diversification.

ANOTHER SOLUTION TO DOING WELL FINANCIALLY: RISK TAKING AND HARD WORK

If clouds are full of water,
  they pour rain on the earth.

Whether a tree falls to the south or to the north,
in the place where it falls, there it will lie.
Whoever watches the wind will not plant;
whoever looks at the clouds will not reap.

As you do not know the path of the wind,
or how the body is formed in a mother's womb,
so you cannot understand the work of God,
the Maker of all things.

Sow your seed in the morning,
and at evening let your hands not be idle,
for you do not know which will succeed,
whether this or that,
or whether both will do equally well. (Ecclesiastes 11:3-6)

Have you ever stared at the clouds and wondered if it will rain later that day? Have you ever thought about the path of the wind? We are naturally fearful of things we cannot control and don't fully understand. When it comes to investing, we can sit and wait for the perfect conditions before we try. But we all know there's no reward without some risk. Solomon encourages us to get busy and take a chance (in a diversified way). Don't get caught up in the "paralysis of analysis!"

There's just a lot that we don't know. Even though we know a lot more these days about gestation and weather patterns, we still haven't figured out how to forecast the future. We don't know if our day job or night job will be more prosperous. We don't know which investment we make will succeed and which won't. But if we spread out our investments enough, we can withstand the inevitable failures of some of those investments.

It's natural to take it easy and not really apply ourselves to what we are doing, because we're not sure how it will benefit us. It's physically, mentally and emotionally easier not to apply ourselves. Joseph is a great example of someone who did his best even when the situation did not look favorable. He had various low-level jobs like shepherd boy, house slave, and head prisoner. God used those roles to shape him into the fabulously wealthy ruler of a powerful nation.

Hard work is just as important for our investments as it is for our careers. When we make a serious effort to diversify, we gain the benefit of understanding our investments on a deeper level. After all, how can we make good decisions about things we don't understand? Diversifying, by its nature, helps us to consider and prepare for the future. Although diversifying takes effort, it is energy well spent.

A GREEDY MINDSET MAKES YOU A BAD INVESTOR

"Watch out! Be on your guard against all kinds of greed; life does not consist in an abundance of possessions."
(Luke 12:15)

Just admit it: you're greedy! We all are. It's part of the human condition. The sooner you admit it to yourself, the sooner you can prioritize the things that really matter. Not only does greed lead you down the wrong road spiritually, but it works against you when you invest.

Good planning and hard work lead to prosperity,
 but hasty shortcuts lead to poverty. (Proverbs 21:5 NLT)

Greed makes you take risky shortcuts that usually end up hurting you. It can also make you take larger risks than you should. Sometimes it can suck you into "get-rich-quick schemes," which typically promise huge amounts of money for minimal work.

Granted, you might hear that you must work hard at first to "build your downline." But then you are promised that you can bask in the riches that will come from the residual income from your downline's downline. You'll probably learn about "small investments" you have to make for training or to purchase starter products. You'll certainly hear about examples of those in the organization who are getting very rich. What you may not realize is that they are getting rich off people like you.

Those who work their land will have abundant food,
 but those who chase fantasies will have their fill of poverty.

A faithful person will be richly blessed,
 but one eager to get rich will not go unpunished.
(Proverbs 28:19-20)

I had a friend who got involved in a house flipping scheme, where he would buy an expensive house at the direction of a company. The company was supposed to pay his mortgage payments until it could provide a buyer who would pay much more than the purchase price. Of course, the payments stopped quickly and there was no buyer. I spent the better part of a Saturday helping him redo the floors in his investment home so he could immediately sell it at a loss before his finances were completely destroyed.

A fool and his money are quickly parted. —Old English Proverb

There's a sucker born every minute. —Unknown

If it sounds too good to be true, it probably is! Think of all the smart, rich people that were duped by Bernie Madoff. Intelligence is no match for greed. Don't be fooled by promises of easy wealth and don't let greed make you ignore common sense. Whether it's multi-level marketing or a too-good-to-be-true investment, don't fall for the scam. God's plan involves hard work and diversification.

PATIENCE LEADS TO WEALTH

Dishonest money dwindles away,
  But whoever gathers money little by little makes it grow.
(Proverbs 13:11)

Whenever I see an exotic sports car, I usually want to see who is at the wheel. Most of the time, I see a grayed man in his 60s, which is a bit anticlimactic, but not surprising. Anyone who is middle aged knows that wealth is built steadily over time. For those who are younger: have patience!

There are tons of articles out there about how you can become a millionaire with simple saving and investing strategies. It's just simple math; the key is to start young and save steadily. Here are some practical rules for building wealth steadily.

1) Have a steady stream of income and build from there. For most of us, that means getting a job (and keeping it!), preferably one that pays well and has the potential for advancement. Keep in mind that even if you are not able to earn much, you can always figure ways to lower your expenses.

2) Invest only what you can afford to lose, never more. You don't

want to get into debt or have large setbacks.

3) Invest in small chunks into diversified (non-correlated) assets. We will discuss various options in the next few chapters.

4) Make sure your lifestyle isn't inflating too fast. This is where most people's wealth building plans get derailed. It's very hard to reduce your standard of living once you've upped it. Just as saving over time can add up, so can spending over time.

ONLY ENTRUST MONEY TO THOSE WHO HAVE EXPERTISE & GET ADVICE FROM KNOWLEDGEABLE PEOPLE

Gold slippeth away from the man who invests it in business or purposes with which he is not familiar or which are not approved by those skilled in its keep.
—*The Richest Man in Babylon* (George S. Clason)[53]

Over the years, you'll come across many investment opportunities. Some will come from those who don't really know what they are doing. The offer might even come from a relative who has a "business idea." If they don't have experience in the type of investment, don't invest! If you must, put in very little and expect to never see the money again.

When you invest, do it with people who have expertise in whatever business you are investing in. When you get specific investment advice, make sure the advisor is qualified. Keep in mind that financial advisors operate on a for-profit basis. It's usually better to get advice from someone who charges a flat fee, rather than someone who makes commissions of off your investments. Their advice will tend to be less biased.

They are there to make money off of you, so their financial interests will take precedence over yours. Sad to say that not all professionals can be trusted, so you need to go one step further. Get advice from others!

Plans fail for lack of counsel,
but with many advisers they succeed. (Proverbs 15:22)

Don't just talk to one person. Talk to lots of people; preferably people who know you and your situation. Talk to members of your church who have expertise. Call knowledgeable relatives. Have lunch with business associates. Embrace conflicting views. If you have an idea or plan, advisors may not change your mind, but they can still affect how you approach things. Be open to what people have to tell you, but ultimately make your own decision.

HOW DIVERSIFIED SHOULD I BE?

The only thing that is constant is change.
—Paraphrase from Heraclitus[54]

In a world where the economy is stable, you only need a moderate amount of diversification. In a financially insecure world, you want increased diversification. In my humble opinion, the world economy is in very uncertain times.

The economic world of the late 20th century which provided increasing wealth for all in the Western World has gradually shifted in the other direction, except for the very wealthiest. The change has been slow enough that it could almost be ignored. With low wage gains, greater job instability, and a higher cost of living, most feel the weight of the economy closing in on all sides.

> In a financially insecure world, you want increased diversification. In my humble opinion, the world economy is in very uncertain times.

Many people have the bulk of their wealth in their home and their 401(k) or IRA. So, is having a diversified portfolio within your 401(k) good enough? Most people's retirement accounts consist of stocks and bonds contained in mutual funds. A variety of stocks and bonds, while in a sense can be diversified, is really too narrow to be truly diversified.

In 2008, the world's financial system nearly collapsed. If that had occurred, stock and bond holders would have been left with pennies on the dollar. Ironically, people view Wall Street investments as safe, despite its reputation for fraud and volatility. Also, if you look closely at housing prices, you can see that they are highly correlated with the stock market. Stock markets and housing have been moving in tandem.

Many might counter by saying that the market crashes of 2001 and 2008 were only temporary and that the market generally goes up and performs very well. I would only agree that that has been the case in recent history. If you look at the following 100-year Dow Jones Industrial Average (DJIA) chart,[55] you can see that a major uptrend started in the 1980s.

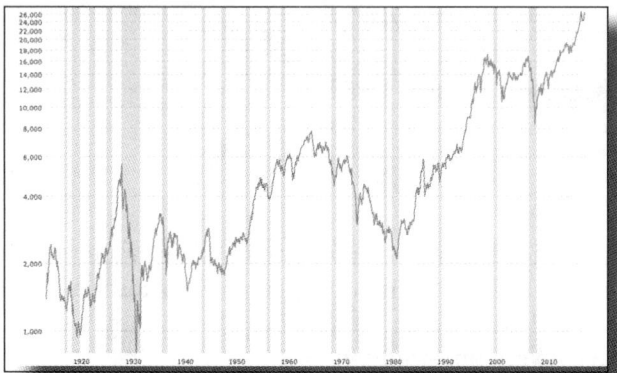

There were many long periods of time that the stock market was not a great investment:
1) Sep 1929 to Jan 1959 (about 30 years) to break even
2) Feb 1966 to June 1995 (about 30 years) to break even
3) Dec 1999 to Nov 2013 (about 14 years) to break even

Of course, the DJIA has moved up dramatically over the 100-year period, but that doesn't mean that your money couldn't just as easily get stuck in the doldrums for 30 years, especially if you buy at peaks. Do we look like we might be close to a peak now? The stock market has been generally great since the mid-90s, but only God knows when that trend will change. Seasoned investors know that nothing ever moves up in a straight line.

There are many other investments that a person can own in order to diversify off of Wall Street. How broadly diversified should you be? I think that should reflect your belief in the stability of the stock market and financial system. No matter how bullish you are on the stock market or housing, you should be somewhat diversified just in case.

UNDERSTAND YOUR INVESTOR PROFILE

To invest at your best, you need to understand yourself and your situation. There are many different ways you can invest, so it's just a matter of finding what is right for you and your situation. What is your investor profile?

Most people with retirement accounts are looking for capital appreciation (increase in stock prices). For some, trading stocks may fit; for others, it could be starting a business. Some might like the regular income of rental properties, dividend stocks or bonds. Others may need the perceived safety of cash or stable blue-chip stocks. You most likely want a combination of investments in order to diversify.

Here are some basic questions to consider in evaluating your investor profile:

1. What is your time horizon? In other words: when will you need your money back from the investment? If you plan to retire soon, you have a short time horizon. In that case, you wouldn't want too many volatile investments. If you are young, you have a long time horizon. You are probably in a good position to make long-term investments.

2. What is your risk appetite/aversion? Although this is, to some degree, a function of your time horizon, it's really based on your personality. Some people just can't stand risk. You have to be able to sleep at night. The amount of debt you have (how leveraged you are) should tend toward making you risk averse. Also, the more diversified your income streams, the more risk you can handle (e.g. two income families vs. a single earner).

3. What is your income/tax status? Higher incomes mean higher taxes. At times, tax implications can affect how you might invest.

4. How much time and effort are you willing to put into your investments? Whenever you make an investment, you have to consider the time involved. If it takes too much time, the investment may not be worth what it first appears.

EPILOGUE: THE WIFE OF NOBLE CHARACTER

If you aren't yet convinced that diversified hard work and investments are wise, please look at these selections from the "Wife of Noble Character."

A wife of noble character who can find?
She is worth far more than rubies.
...

*She selects wool and flax
    and works with eager hands.
...
She considers a field and buys it;
    out of her earnings she plants a vineyard.
She sets about her work vigorously;
    her arms are strong for her tasks.
She sees that her trading is profitable,
    and her lamp does not go out at night.
In her hand she holds the distaff
    and grasps the spindle with her fingers.
...
She makes linen garments and sells them,
    and supplies the merchants with sashes.
...
She watches over the affairs of her household
    and does not eat the bread of idleness*

(Proverbs 31:10-27 selections)

Chapter 12

Wall Street Investments

One of the funny things about the stock market is that every time one person buys, another sells, and both think they are astute. —William Feather[56]

Stock exchanges have become the general public's main avenue for investing. If you want to buy $10 or $10,000,000 of stocks or other financial instruments, stock exchanges around the world can accommodate you. You can trade 24/7 with the push of a button.

The stock market (a.k.a. equity market) refers to a collection of stock exchanges where you can issue, buy or sell stocks and other financial instruments. In the U.S., public corporations list their shares for trading under the supervision of the U.S. Securities and Exchange Commission (SEC). The SEC regulates the U.S. markets and enforces laws to minimize fraud and other unfair practices.

In theory, an individual investor has an equal chance to profit on the stock market, but it is well known that professional investors have a significant edge. These professionals work for hedge funds, commercial banks, institutions or other investment groups. With experience, size, liquidity, high frequency trading machines, and smart trading algorithms, you are outmanned and outgunned!

The stock market has delivered excellent returns for most over long periods of time. I have had my fair share of experience with various types of investing and trading on the stock market.[57] In today's financial world, every kind of investment is either in or somehow connected to stock markets.

STOCKS, ETFs, AND MUTUAL FUNDS: THE INVESTMENTS OF CHOICE IN THE WESTERN WORLD

Man is an animal that makes bargains: no other animal does this - no dog exchanges bones with another.
—Adam Smith[58]

What is a stock? Stock is an ownership interest in a company. Each unit of ownership interest is called a share. Companies can have different types of shares and a different number of shares for each type. Typically, the "common stock" of a company is what is traded in public stock exchanges.

Stock investors generally seek capital appreciation, which happens when the value of the company increases. The perceived increase in value is generally reflected in an increasing stock price. The stock can eventually be sold later at a higher value. Some stocks pay cash dividends. A dividend is payment made by a company to its shareholders. Typically, dividends are paid periodically based on a company's profits.

As a purchaser of stock, you do not directly bear the risks of the company. This allows you to reap the benefits of a profitable company without liability or being involved in the day-to-day work of a company. However, you do bear the risk that your stock value will fall (capital depreciation) or fall to zero (due to bankruptcy).

What are mutual funds? A mutual fund is a professionally managed investment fund that pools money from many investors to purchase securities (e.g. stocks and bonds). It's a way of owning a basket of stocks without having to individually purchase each stock. For example, one share of a mutual fund could consist of 100 different stocks.

Similarly, an Exchange Traded Fund (ETF) holds a pool of securities but is not actively managed. ETFs have been shown repeatedly to outperform mutual funds. In other words, the professional managers generally cannot outperform the market as a whole. ETF management fees are very small compared to mutual funds. As a result, more and more investors are choosing ETFs.

Both mutual funds and ETFs offer built in degrees of diversification. Each prospectus (a formal legal description of the fund or ETF) will state that "past performance does not guarantee future results." You may choose a fund based on its past performance, but that doesn't mean it will continue to perform that way in the future. Past performance alone is a flawed way of choosing which mutual funds to invest in.

HOW DO YOU CHOOSE?

Many people have exposure to mutual funds or ETFs through their company's 401(k) or similar plan. How you choose should depend on your investment profile. Many plan offerings have a mutual fund that is based on your projected retirement age. The closer you are to retirement, the more conservative the fund.

> *Markets are driven by fear and greed.*
> —Old Wall Street Wisdom

> *The market can remain irrational longer than you can remain solvent.* —Old Wall Street Wisdom sometimes attributed to John Maynard Keynes

So, how do you pick stocks? That's the real question, isn't it? If anyone actually knew how to successfully do that, that person could just trade their way to enormous wealth. You can go with your gut or just guess. You can get a stock tip from a friend or online, but that's not really investing. There are two major types of analysis that stock investors engage in: fundamental and technical analysis.

Fundamental analysis involves studying the companies and the business trends that might affect those companies. For instance, you might believe that the recent hiring of a particular CEO is good for a company, so you buy shares. There are several problems with this type of investing for an individual investor. First, you are usually the last to know the news that might affect the stock price.

Second, whatever information is out there is already "priced in" to the share price. In other words, you are effectively guessing about trends or outcomes, effectively speculating or gambling. Worse yet, when you hear the news later than others, you might react after all the "smart money" has already reacted. Retail investors typically buy at the end of rallies and sell close to bottoms, leaving themselves with the short end of the stick.[59]

> *Sometimes your best investments are the ones you don't make.* —Donald Trump[60]

Some investors turn to technical analysis, which involves using patterns in market data to predict future price movements. You might have heard technical analysis terms like support, resistance, retracements, trend lines, moving averages and Fibonacci ratios. This type of analysis takes lots of time and effort.

Active trading can be very difficult. Studies show that active individual traders rarely beat the market. Why? For starters, equities trading is essentially a zero-sum game. Sure, the whole market can rise, but to actively trade means that you are trying to make money off of buying and selling in relatively short time periods of time. Retail investors are competing against pros, many of whom use high frequency trading machines with advanced trading algorithms.

> *I will tell you the secret to getting rich on Wall Street. You try to be greedy when others are fearful. And you try to be fearful when others are greedy.* —Warren Buffett[61]

The other reason it's tough to make money actively trading is that investing has a very strong psychological component. Most people are not good at controlling it. People tend to buy high and sell low. Even though it doesn't make sense, we all have an instinct to do it. When we see a stock flying high and everyone is talking about it, we buy in because we get excited and greedy. When we see a stock falling rapidly, we get afraid and sell. Fighting this instinct is very difficult.

> *I can calculate the movement of stars, but not the madness of men.* —Sir Isaac Newton[62]

So, for most people, buying stocks (or mutual funds/ETFs) for the long run is preferable to active trading. This is the trading strategy known as "buy and hold." Keep in mind that buying and holding has its risks as well. If you buy when the market is high and then it drops, it could be many years until you get back to even.

When entering investments, it is typically a good idea to enter them incrementally over time and not all at once. This well-known strategy is known as "dollar cost averaging." Buying in this way reduces short-term price risk. This is another important form of diversification that can help you when building long-term investing positions.

BONDS, CDs, AND INTEREST-BEARING ACCOUNTS: YOU BECOME A LENDER

Bonds are debt investments. When you buy a bond, you effectively lend money to the bond issuer and receive interest over a fixed period. Unlike a stock, you have no ownership stake in the bond issuer. Instead, you become a creditor. There are many types of bonds: municipal, state, sovereign, corporate, junk, etc. The bonds are given a value and traded like stocks. So, although bonds are very different than stocks, they can take on market swings much like stocks.

Bonds are usually more conservative than stocks, but it depends on the bond. If you buy a "junk bond," you get a higher interest rate, because the borrowing entity's credit rating is junk. You take a significant risk you will not get all your money back. This is called default risk. As of the time of writing this book, $74 billion in Puerto Rican bonds are set to be devalued in the largest municipal default in history. Even when a borrowing entity doesn't default, but its credit is downgraded, the corresponding bond value drops.

Another factor that affects bond pricing are general interest rates. Imagine that you bought a municipal bond which carried a 3% return, at a time when savings accounts only offered 1% return. Later, what do you think the bond would be worth if savings accounts also offered 3% returns? The reverse is also true: as interest rates fall, existing bond values rise.

An interest-bearing account is when you loan a bank or other financial entity money and it pays you interest. The bank or financial entity then goes out and invests the money to make higher returns. An interest-bearing account or savings account earns a variable, low interest rate, but is relatively safe because it is insured by the FDIC. What most people do not know is that any money you put in the bank is actually treated as a loan to the bank—even when you earn no interest on it!

A CD or certificate of deposit is similar to an interest-bearing account but has a fixed term and a fixed interest rate. You typically earn higher rates than an interest-bearing account, but you lose the flexibility of accessing it during the loan term. It is also relatively safe and insured by the FDIC. These types of financial instruments are good for emergency funds and holding cash. The only problem with CDs and interest-bearing accounts is that you usually earn very little interest, typically less than the rate of inflation.

RETIREMENT ACCOUNTS: GOVERNMENT SPONSORED SAVINGS

Retirement accounts are not specific financial investments, but rather accounts that are treated differently for tax purposes. These accounts can contain financial investments and take the form of 401(k)s, Individual Retirement Accounts (IRAs), or something similar.

If you don't live in the U.S., you may have a similar type of tax relief in your country.

The basic idea is that you don't pay tax on the money placed into these accounts now, but you only pay the tax when you withdraw the money in retirement. Because your taxable income is likely to be less in retirement, the net tax savings can be significant. Another benefit is that any earnings in the account grows tax free until withdrawn. Here's the catch: you can't withdraw funds until you are 59½ or you will face a 10% penalty and income tax liability for that year.

> You can save even more money with ROTHs than traditional retirement accounts. This is a great vehicle for keeping an emergency fund, because you can withdraw your principal anytime without penalty.

These types of accounts are essentially modern-day pensions. The big differences are that you control the investments and you aren't guaranteed a set payment for life. Most companies' 401(k)s give you a limited menu of mutual fund choices. In IRAs, you can fully control your investments. After you are 59 ½, you can take out as much money as you would like. However, you are taxed on any withdrawals.

When your employer subsidizes you by matching your 401(k) contribution, you should almost always contribute up to that amount, even when you are in debt. If you have bad debt, you would normally focus on that first, but this "free-money" situation is a notable exception.

ROTH IRAs AND 401(k)s

Unlike the traditional versions of these accounts, for ROTHs you pay your tax upfront. The advantage is that you are not taxed later, and you won't pay tax on the earnings. You can save even more money with ROTHs than traditional retirement accounts. This is a great vehicle for keeping an emergency fund, because you can withdraw your principal anytime without penalty. In some special cases, you can even withdraw your earnings early without penalty.

EDUCATION SAVINGS ACCOUNTS: 529 PLANS AND COVERDELL (FEDERAL) PLANS

Much like ROTH IRAs, the U.S. government has allowed you to defer paying tax on earnings in these plan accounts. If used for qualified educational expenses, the proceeds can be withdrawn tax free! The Coverdell program is national, while 529 programs are state specific.[63] Each program has different advantages and disadvantages. If you are interested, please investigate your state's program.

Chapter 13

Other Investments

Before there were modern financial markets like Wall Street, the world hummed with commerce. It may not have moved as quickly, but it was much more tangible. There's a lot more to wealth than gyrating stock prices on a computer screen.

This chapter covers a wide array of investments, which are not in any particular order. Some of these categories are not traditionally considered investments, but I have included them because they can have a significant effect on your long-term finances.

EDUCATION, TRAINING AND SKILLS: INVESTING IN YOURSELF

Education is a lifetime investment, which includes traditional degree programs, vocational training, apprenticeships, certifications, informal learning, etc.[64] The *Hamilton Project* says that college graduates earn an average of $1,200,000 over their careers.[65] Those with only a high school diploma earn about half that amount. Because college is so well known to be a good investment, I won't belabor the point. Instead, I'll spend the rest of this section explaining how that dynamic is changing and what you should focus on.

When I first went to college in 1990, my tuition was a pleasant $600 per semester. Now, in-state tuition at my alma matter is about ten times that figure. The average class of 2017 graduate had $39,400 in student loan debt, up 6% from the year before.[66] As of mid-2018, outstanding U.S. student loan debt had exceeded 1.5 trillion dollars.[67] These figures are rising at an alarming and unsustainable pace. I say all this not to scare you or your loved ones from going to college. I say this to make sure your eyes are open and that you really look closely at whether your educational plans make sense.

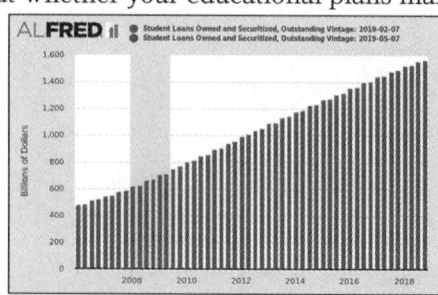

Outstanding Student Loans
(owned and securitized)[68]

Based on the *Hamilton Project* statistics, it seems that anyone who wants to do well financially should pursue a higher education. Statistics, however, can be very deceiving. Isn't it entirely possible that highly motivated, smart people tend to go to college, which means that it was the person and not the college who actually produced the higher earnings?[69] Also, these statistics do not account for the cost of education and all the interest that would be paid upon it if borrowed, which has become quite ominous.

Granted, many lucrative professions require a formal education (e.g. doctor, lawyer, C.P.A.). As well, most hiring managers for non-licensed professional roles will only consider those with a college diploma. But many other lucrative professions do not require a diploma (e.g. business owner, computer programmer, machinist). There are many ways to earn a solid income.

For those determined to go to college—keep in mind that lifetime earnings vary greatly by your field of study. Fields of study that involve computation

You should invest in education but do it sensibly. Pursue a college degree for a paying career, not for intellectual stimulation.

tend to earn much more than others (e.g. science, technology, engineering, mathematics, accounting and economics).[70] That pay gap is widening more and more with time.

Am I saying that college isn't worth it for some? Yes, I am absolutely making that point. You've got to look at career prospects and match that against the debt you would accumulate to get there. This can be hard for some to hear, because higher education carries a prestige and accomplishment value. When someone asks you where you went to college, you want to be able to give a good answer. Sure, college can help with your self-confidence, but is it worth it?

No doubt, finishing a degree program is a tremendous accomplishment. Much like finishing high school, it is the culmination of many years of hard work and determination. But unlike high school, college isn't free. College isn't solely a means to an end, but I submit that it is *mostly* a means to an end.[71]

Again, I am not trying to discourage people from investing in an education. You should invest in education but do it sensibly. Pursue a college degree for a paying career, not for intellectual stimulation. If it is wisdom, mental growth or learning you seek, there are many ways keep your mind busy that are free or very inexpensive. Consider free or inexpensive online sources for learning, certificates or even degrees. Look for value, not prestige. You don't need college to be well-read or intellectual.

Would you pay double or triple for your degree simply because you want to go to an out-of-state college?[72] Would you pay double to go to a slightly more prestigious school? In the days when tuition was $600 a semester, such decisions were much more trivial. Now, when faced with tuition ten to forty times that amount, you really need to think long and hard about such decisions.[73]

I also don't want to discourage people from choosing professions they may love, just because they are not high paying. I just want you to find a program that makes sense for you. If you aren't in it for the money, then why not find a program that won't put you in too much debt and force you worry about money later?

GRADUATE SCHOOL AND PROFESSIONAL PROGRAMS

Of making many books there is no end, and much study wearies the body. (Ecclesiastes 12:12b)

As I was wrapping up my Psychology degree, I wasn't sure where I wanted to go from there. My undergraduate degree did not afford me a path to gainful employment or experience, so I didn't want to get a job while taking my time to consider my next move. After a short period of reflection and some advice from a friend, I decided to go to law school.

When you commit to law school or any involved career path, you set yourself on a track that is difficult to get off of. Although things have more or less worked out for me, I have often had second thoughts about my choices. I hadn't done my due diligence. I hadn't spoken with lawyers or researched the industry enough. I wish I had taken more time to think things through. Better yet, I wish I had been exploring my options from a much younger age.

I have met many lawyers who feel trapped by their professions, because of the time and financial investment they put into it. By the time law students graduate and pass the bar exam, many have over $150,000 in debt. The entire process takes at least three years, not including applying for law school. Many lawyers don't pursue the types of careers they really want because they are forced to choose a job that pays enough to service their school debt.

In my dark days of debt while living in Silicon Valley (see my

"Deep Dark Debt Hole" story in Chapter 3), I considered becoming a patent attorney, in order to keep up with the Joneses. The only problem was that I did not have an engineering degree, which is basically a requirement of succeeding in the field. After calculating the additional costs of getting another degree on top of my existing debt, I concluded that it would put me in a nearly impossible amount of debt, even if I were to be gainfully employed.

The pressure of education debt is even threatening the venerable practice of medicine. While many nurses and physician's assistants have done quite well for themselves, this is much less true for newer doctors. It is very common for medical students to graduate with over $200,000 in debt. After four rigorous years of medical school, most graduates must endure a two-year residency with relatively low pay. At the age of twenty-seven or higher, new doctors begin the process of paying down their massive debt. How badly do you want to become a doctor?[74]

Graduate school can become the option of choice for those who are not sure what they want to do. It can solidify a person's achievements and sometimes provide a path to gainful employment. But sometimes, it can just become expensive wallpaper. Don't get an M.B.A. just because you aren't sure what else to do. If your employer will subsidize your M.B.A. and give you an automatic raise upon completion, then by all means. Remember to research the path you are interested in pursuing and think in terms of value.

HOME OWNERSHIP: A PLACE TO LIVE OR AN INVESTMENT?

Put your outdoor work in order
  and get your fields ready;
after that, build your house. (Proverbs 24:27)

This proverb reminds us that we need to focus on our regular income—and that our home building is secondary. But if we have the money and want to buy a home, how should we view it? Is it an expense, like a car? Or is it an investment, like a stock?

Common wisdom says that buying a home for yourself is the best investment a person can make. Consistently rising home prices and sizeable government tax breaks on mortgage interest have bolstered this idea. However, there's a real debate going on these days over whether a home is a good path toward building wealth.[75] In the

U.S., the new 2018 tax laws have doubled the standard deduction and limited state and local tax itemized deductions, rendering the home mortgage interest deduction useless to many Americans.

If you really think about it, a home is much like a car. It's made of materials that deteriorate over time. Roofs and decks need replacing. It is connected to machines that need regular repair and replacement like HVAC units, garage doors, plumbing and water heaters. Eventually, the home itself will be torn down and replaced. If you've owned a home for any length of time, you understand this burden.

On the other hand, home values have dramatically risen over time. The average price of a home in the U.S. in 1964 was $20,500![76] Keep in mind that the average home was much more modest in 1964 than the average home today. The average price in 1985 was $100,800. The average price in 2010 was $272,900. The average price in April 2018 was $407,300.[77]

However, this dynamic is more of a recent phenomenon. The Case-Schiller 100-year housing index shows little increase in values from 1900-1945, a time with relatively low inflation. The increase in modern home values, in my opinion, are mostly a function of inflation and an increase in square footage. Another factor to keep in mind are all the costs of homeownership, which include purchase transaction costs, interest on mortgages, taxes, insurance, maintenance, improvement and selling costs. I conclude that while home values are a hedge against inflation, the increase is roughly offset by all the associated costs.

Granted, we all need a place to live and will end up paying rent if we don't own. Owning subjects you to the swings of the housing market, while renting subjects you to the swings of the rental market. They are related but are actually two different markets. The housing market is much more volatile and has higher stakes than the rental market. Let me give you an example.

When my wife and I moved to Los Angeles County in 2002, we rented a modest apartment for a relatively modest price. We were able to live comfortably and save money, little by little. After a couple years of living there, I saw a home-buying mania develop. Everywhere I looked, there were mortgage advertisements. Just about everyone I talked to said we should buy a home, even people in my church.

In late 2003, we finally did a little home shopping. I felt like everything we looked at was outrageously expensive. I was genuinely shocked and couldn't understand how people across the city

could afford to buy. When I explained to people that I believed all the homes were too expensive, I would hear things like:
"You better buy before it becomes more expensive!"
"Home prices have never gone down before."
"If you can't afford it, you can always sell your house at a profit."

I just didn't buy it, literally and figuratively. After doing the math, it just didn't make sense; and not just for me, but for everyone buying at that time. We were saving thousands of dollars each month by renting, even when accounting for tax breaks and equity gains. The rest was history. It turns out that housing prices can go down.

> When buying a home with mortgage financing, I recommend getting a fixed-rate loan. Although you pay a higher rate at first, the fixed-rate loan shields you from rising interest rates.

A few years later, I worked at a firm defending mortgage loan servicers (commercial litigation) against various claims. Many of the lawsuits were frivolous, made by desperate homeowners who couldn't make their mortgage payments. Most couldn't sell their homes, because their home values were underwater. Most were foreclosed on and forced to leave.

I heard many sob stories, but the truth is that most of those borrowers should never have bought their homes in the first place. I saw many "liar's loans" in which income was falsified and ignored by underwriters.[78] The loan applications would typically contain an unspecified source of income for $10,000 or so per month. My favorite loan application that I saw was made by a Domino's Pizza employee making $10 per hour for a $350,000 home. Everyone in the law firm office had a good laugh about that one.

The point is that housing prices *can* fluctuate and can be dangerous to your finances if you cannot afford it. Even if home prices don't fall, you can get into a jam if you lose your main source of income. When you make the affordability calculations, be sure to realistically account for all the expenses. Be sure to get advice from knowledgeable people.

When buying a home with mortgage financing, I recommend getting a fixed-rate loan. Although you pay a higher rate at first, the fixed-rate loan shields you from rising interest rates. In most cases, it isn't worth the risk to use a variable-rate loan. If mortgage interest rates fall significantly, you can always refinance your loan. If interest rates rise, then your payment will not be affected.

Much like with education, I am not trying to discourage anyone from buying, but I want you to be careful and think value. Owning a house can be great. I own a house. Here's a list of things to consider when making that decision.

Should You Buy A House?
Lots of advantages:
1. Sense of ownership and a chance to truly nest (more of a psychological benefit)
2. Selection of school district
3. Possible tax savings (mortgage interest tax deduction)
4. Built in savings through equity building (more psychological benefit)
5. Inflation hedge
6. Chance for capital appreciation[79]

Should You Buy A House?
Lots of disadvantages:
1. Risk of foreclosure for failing to pay the mortgage (some states even allow for deficiency judgments)
2. High maintenance costs (both money and effort)
3. Property taxes and insurance
4. Realtor fees and sale costs
5. Tying up net worth in single asset (creating a lack of diversification)
6. Chance for a net capital loss

Be sure to do plenty of research and get lots of advice. If we get advice on smaller matters, why not get advice on what is likely to be the largest purchase in your lifetime? Bottom line is: don't bite off more than you can chew!

> *"Suppose one of you wants to build a tower. Won't you first sit down and estimate the cost to see if you have enough money to complete it? For if you lay the foundation and are not able to finish it, everyone who sees it will ridicule you, saying, 'This person began to build and wasn't able to finish.'"* (Luke 14:28-30)

Of course, this passage is really about deciding to follow Jesus, but keep in mind that Jesus was a carpenter and had likely seen a few underfunded projects. If you don't finish the tower, does it have economic value? Probably not. So, the tower investor would have used up all his or her money and would be ruined financially, all because he or she didn't properly estimate the cost of the investment.

To drive the point home, I want to introduce you to a statistical concept: The Gambler's Ruin.

THE GAMBLER'S RUIN AND BEING OVER-LEVERAGED IN HOUSING

> *Gambler's ruin is that a persistent gambler with finite wealth, playing a fair game (that is, each bet has expected value zero to both sides) will eventually and inevitably go broke against an opponent with infinite wealth.*[80]

We all have a finite amount of wealth. The "house" so to speak, has relatively infinite wealth. We cannot keep playing (investing) if we lose what we have to play (invest) with. Much like a casino game, there's always risk involved when making investments. In short, our limited wealth is a huge hindrance when it comes to investing.

This helps explain why you rarely win when you are low on chips in Texas Hold'em. The other players with more chips can bully you around, because they can afford to lose hands and still be around to play another hand. You, on the other hand, have to be careful and often pass up opportunities to see "the flop." Even if you win a hand, the win is relatively small, because you have less to bet with.

What does this have to do with buying a house? Well, it should have nothing to do with it, except that the housing market takes great swings on national, regional and local levels. So, even though you shouldn't think of your house as an investment, it takes on the risk characteristics of an investment. This risk should be taken into consideration.

For example, a woman buys a $400,000 house, when she really should have bought a $200,000 house. Maybe she could technically afford it, but if she loses her job, she could get foreclosed on, because she is underwater on the house. She would probably have little equity in the house, because she would have made a tiny down payment. She wouldn't have time to sell it, because she would have no savings to buy time to make the sale. She would have no savings, because all her excess dollars went to the house and she would end up losing everything.

What if she bought the $200,000 house? There, she could have made a bigger down payment relative to the price of the house. She would likely have gotten a better interest rate. She would have likely been able to save, for example, $500 per month to put into her emergency fund. So, when she lost her job, she would have had time to sell it, and walk away with decent credit and cash in hand so that she could rent a place to live.

Even if you never face foreclosure, you can still lose or tie up large sums of wealth in a home. This is money that cannot be otherwise invested. Remember, if you don't have money (or access to it), you can't make investment returns. So, consider carefully what kind of home you purchase.

In short, you should have both the wealth and the liquidity to withstand market swings. Don't get over-leveraged, which means that you've borrowed too much money; similarly, make sure that you don't take out a home equity loan to finance an expensive lifestyle that cannot be sustained in the long run. Be careful; it's very easy to oversize your life, leaving little room for savings and generosity.

RENTAL AND INVESTMENT PROPERTY

> *But land is land, and it's safer than the stocks and bonds of Wall Street swindlers.* —Eugene O'Neill[81]

Owning rental property is one of the most tried and true paths to building wealth. After all, everyone needs a place to live. Why not rent it to them? Similarly, businesses need physical space. Even one of the most popular board games of all time, Monopoly, is based on acquiring properties and renting space in order to bankrupt other players.

> **Be careful; it's very easy to oversize your life, leaving little room for savings and generosity.**

The author of the popular financial book *Rich Dad, Poor Dad*, Robert Kiyosaki, made his fortune through rental properties.[82] The most basic premise in his financial philosophy is that you want assets, not liabilities. He defines assets as things that put money in your pocket without working. So, a rental property is an asset, but your personal home is a liability, because it costs you money.

I personally don't view owning rental property as black and white as Robert Kiyosaki does. There is work involved in owning and managing rental properties. For owners of small rental properties, I view it as having a side job or second job.[83] You can't just buy property and rack up rent like in Monopoly. You must be concerned with acquiring and possibly evicting tenants, property maintenance, compliance with landlord's legal duties and increased accounting.

On the other hand, there are many built-in advantages to owning rental properties. As previously discussed, real estate acts as hedge against inflation. You're able to take advantage of tax deductions like depreciation. Profits from rental properties tend to be slow, but steady. And years later when you're ready to sell the property, you are likely to have a significant pay day.

Rental properties are a very different type of investment than flipping homes. Flipping homes is a high-risk endeavor that is best left to the pros. I suppose if you are really interested in becoming a pro, you can try it out. In that case, I recommend starting with a very modest project. There's a huge difference between sitting on a couch watching HGTV and putting your money and time into house flipping!

Buying empty land for future sale is typically a very long-term play. Keep in mind that you will have to pay property taxes and possibly insurance on the land for years before seeing any payday. If you aren't very wealthy and interested in this, you may want to consider having a small stake in with other investors.

For the record, timeshares aren't an investment. Don't let anyone tell you otherwise. Timeshares aren't even a good value, unless you are sure you are going to consistently use them. For those who want a timeshare, I recommend buying them on the secondary market. Vacation homes can possibly be a hybrid timeshare and investment. Be very careful when thinking about buying a timeshare or vacation home.

OTHER BUSINESSES OR OWNING YOUR OWN BUSINESS

This isn't a book about starting your own business, although there is crossover between business and investing. There's no end to the various ways you can make (or lose) money in business. You can use your money to invest in your own business or have a partnership with others. You could also become a passive (non-managing) investor in a business.

INSURANCE: THE POOLING OF RESOURCES TO COMBAT UNREASONABLE RISK

Insurance usually conjures to mind unpleasant premium payments and fighting to receive payment on claims. However, at its core, it is really an amazing financial invention. Just as money allows people to store and make wealth portable, insurance allows you to take risks you would not otherwise be able to bear. Take a house for instance. Most people would never own something that expensive if they couldn't protect themselves from the potential loss (e.g. from fire).

Why is this an investment? Well, it is more of a protection from losing what you already have, which is essentially an investment. In the case of life insurance and disability insurance, you protect your loved ones from the loss of your income. If you have dependents, get term-life insurance and disability insurance. Make sure your major assets (home, car, health, etc.) are well insured at competitive premiums. If you have significant wealth to protect, consider having higher coverage limits on your car and home insurance policies.

BASIC EMERGENCY PREPARATIONS

If we are truly going to diversify, shouldn't we prepare for a physical disaster? I'm not talking about Doomsday Preppers; I'm talking about basic survival preparation recommended by national and local governments. The Federal Emergency Management Agency (FEMA) has stated that "[t]he need to prepare is real. ... If a disaster occurs in your community, [the government] will try to help you, but you need to be ready as well."[84]

If you put effort into making basic emergency preparations and never used them, it could seem like a waste. On the other hand, those preparations could be what saves you and your loved ones' lives! FEMA has cited these possible emergencies: floods, tornadoes, winter storms, earthquakes, fires, hazmat incidents, nuclear meltdown, biological/chemical weapon, dirty bomb, E.M.P. and nuclear blast. Recent examples are Hurricanes Harvey, Irma and Maria, which wreaked havoc in Texas, Florida, and the Caribbean. As I am writing now, Hurricane Florence is heading toward the Carolinas.

I think that the last 35 days or so have been a gut

check for Americans that we do not have a true culture of preparedness in this country. And we've got a lot of work to do. Whether it's in education and being ready, it's not just saying, hey, have three days' worth of supplies ready to go. It's greater than that. It's also people having the finances and the savings to be able to overcome simple emergencies. We have to hit the reset button and create a true culture of preparedness starting at a very young age and filtering all the way up. —FEMA Director Brock Long on September 26, 2017[85]

> Ask yourself honestly: if the power went out and stores were out of supplies, how long could you and your family survive on just what you have in your house?

We live in a society that is highly dependent on fragile "just in time" systems. For example, your local grocery store might only have enough food in it to feed the local populous for three days. Before serious winter storms or hurricanes, it is common for store shelves to go bare. In more intense situations, looting can wipe out supplies at stores within minutes.

Ask yourself honestly: if the power went out and stores were out of supplies, how long could you and your family survive on just what you have in your house? If the water went out, how long could you survive? I don't mean to scare anyone, but these are basic things that we have only ignored in recent modern times. Doesn't it make sense to have some basic supplies for you and your family?

Here's a basic list of supplies every family should have on hand:
- Clean drinking water (1 gallon per day per person)
- Food (2000-3000 cal. per day per person) and the ability to cook it if needed
- Ability to keep warm in cold environments
- First aid supplies (most first aid kits are very minimal)
- Family disaster plans
- Flashlight and batteries
- Hand-crank powered radio
- Cash on hand

YOUR HEALTH: SPEND ON IT NOW OR LATER

I'll ask you an honest question: how valuable is your health to you? Although we aren't in control of many things than can happen with our health, we can prevent many common ailments later in life with how we live today. I've heard that sugar is the tobacco of the 21st century. We can control sugar over-consumption and we can make the time to get regular exercise.

A healthy lifestyle takes time, effort and expense, but can be well worth the effort (within reason). Enough said on that.

ESTATE PLANNING: PLANNING BEYOND YOUR DEATH AND OTHER UNFORTUNATE SCENARIOS

A good person leaves an inheritance for their children's children,
but a sinner's wealth is stored up for the righteous.
(Proverbs 13:22)

The last thing most of us want to do is make a will. It forces us to consider our own death and post-mortem affairs, but it is very important for those who outlive us. If you have dependents, you should have life and disability insurance. Remember: death and taxes are certain! A godly person of character considers and puts into effect their estate plans.

Near the cross of Jesus stood his mother, his mother's sister, Mary the wife of Clopas, and Mary Magdalene. When Jesus saw his mother there, and the disciple whom he loved standing nearby, he said to her, "Woman, here is your son," and to the disciple, "Here is your mother." From that time on, this disciple took her into his home. (John 19:25-27)

Jesus—the eldest son in his family—knew he was not going to be around to support his mother, who was a widow. I suspect he wanted her to be in a spiritually nurturing environment, so he passed that responsibility on to his beloved disciple John. For those of us with minor children, we should also consider carefully who would take care of them if you aren't there. Not only should your will make mention of it, but you should talk to the person you intend to have care for your children.

Let me stress that your wealth may not be passed on in a way that you would want, if you don't carefully put together your last will and testament. If you die without a will, your state has a set of rules that govern how your wealth will be distributed. Each state has different rules. I strongly urge everyone reading this to have a will made at the advice of a licensed attorney in your state.

It's not uncommon for families to be torn apart by greed when it comes time to divide up a deceased family member's estate. Greed and bad attitudes exist among family members well before a death, but a good estate plan can greatly minimize any potential drama. A non-existent or poor estate plan can fan the flames of a family's strife.

What if you are physically or mentally incapacitated? Who will make decisions for you and handle your affairs? Each person should consider having both a health and a financial power of attorney created, which would give authority to who you appoint to make important decisions. How your health care is handled, and your money is spent if your health is in rapid decline can have huge implications for your family and wealth.

On a related note, each person should also have an advance directive, which is a way for you to give advance consent to have or withhold certain medical treatments. An advance directive gives you a better chance of having your wishes carried out when you can't talk to the doctors about what you want.

For the very wealthy, estate planning can have tremendous tax implications. A well-made estate plan, possibly involving trusts, can greatly reduce tax liabilities. A trust is a relationship whereby property is held by one party for the benefit of another. Trusts are usually used to: 1) avoid estate taxes, 2) avoid probate, 3) shield wealth from liability and/or 4) control the manner in which property and money is used. Trusts can also be useful in cases of incapacity.

Bottom line, your legacy matters. Your spiritual, emotional and financial legacy are all important and intertwined. Thoughtfully establishing your wealth distribution, health preferences and care for your dependents is wise and righteous.

Chapter 14

Alternative Investments

"I am sending you out like sheep among wolves. Therefore be as shrewd as snakes and as innocent as doves." (Matthew 10:16)

God has no problem with shrewdness. The financial world (and the world in general) is a vicious place filed with wolves. Should we cower? No, we should be as innocent as doves and as shrewd as snakes. We should consider all righteous options, even if they are not in the mainstream. Christianity, in its roots, is not a mainstream religion and we are not bound to conventional thinking.

COUNTERPARTY RISK

There are many reasons why people invest in alternatives like precious metals, cryptocurrencies, fine art and collectibles. They can have an aesthetic or ideological appeal. But the one reason why everyone should consider them is that they can provide protection against counterparty risk. What is counterparty risk?

> *Counterparty risk is the risk to each party of a contract that the counterparty will not live up to its contractual obligations. Counterparty risk is a risk to both parties and should be considered when evaluating a contract. In most financial contracts, counterparty risk is also known as default risk.*
> —Investopedia[86]

You might think that because you aren't contracting with anyone, you are safe from counterparty risk. But what you may not realize is that almost ALL your investments involve counterparty risk, including the currency you use. In fact, many of your investments have multiple layers of counterparty risk surrounding them.

For bonds, it is easy to see the counterparty risk. The interest rate you get is correlated to the bond issuer's default risk. For any bond, there's a chance you may not get paid back in full or at all.

For insurance, there's always a chance you won't get your claim paid because the insurance company goes bust. That's why insurance companies are rated based on their financial stability.[87] U.S. states have funds to pay policyholders in case of insurance company default, but it is limited and not enough to pay claims in the case of a systemic collapse.

Through the Troubled Asset Relief Program (TARP) in 2008, U.S. taxpayers *en masse* bailed out the American International Group (AIG) to keep the entire world financial system from crumbling. If AIG did not get bailed out, it would not be able to pay out on policy claims and many of their policyholders would become insolvent. The failure of AIG to pay its claims nearly started a cataclysmic chain reaction. AIG was too big to fail.

HIGH INFLATION AND HYPERINFLATION

Cast but a glance at riches, and they are gone,
for they will surely sprout wings
and fly off to the sky like an eagle. (Proverbs 23:5)

It's a little harder to understand how currencies (a.k.a. cash) have counterparty risk. In a sense, they don't because they can be produced in unlimited supplies. But they do bear counterparty risk in that they are only as good as people believe they are. If enough people believe currencies are worth less, then they eventually devalue. For example, today a Big Mac might cost $5, but next year you might pay $10, even though beef, buns, cheese and special sauce are in ample supply. In my example, the Big Mac didn't change in value; the currency did.

This phenomenon is known as inflation, which if left unchecked, can lead to hyperinflation. When a currency begins to heavily devalue, people quickly spend all their currency before it loses its value. This quick turnaround (money velocity) is what accelerates the inflation, thereby creating the extreme effect of hyperinflation. For example, the inflation rate for the Venezuelan Bolivar at the end of April 2018 was 17968%.[88] That means the same 5 Bolivar Big Mac in April 2017, costs about 900 Bolivars in April 2018.

Economists believe that hyperinflations are caused by
large persistent government deficits financed primarily by

money creation (rather than by borrowing or by increasing taxation). As such, hyperinflation is often associated with some stress to the government budget, such as wars or their aftermath, sociopolitical upheavals, a collapse in export prices, or other crises that make it difficult for the government to collect tax revenue. A sharp decrease in real tax revenue coupled with a strong need to maintain government spending, together with an inability or unwillingness to borrow, can lead a country into hyperinflation.[89]

Does your country currently exhibit any of the causes of hyperinflation listed above like wars, sociopolitical upheaval, shrinking tax revenues and rampant money creation? As of July 31, 2017, the Federal Reserve owned 12.7% of the U.S.'s public debt. The Federal Reserve is the U.S.'s central bank. So, the U.S. (through the Federal Reserve) is effectively purchasing its own debt in order to artificially keep interest rates low. These "open market operations" are effectively creating more currency and creating the risk of heavy inflation.

Both inflationary and deflationary spirals are devasting to economies and people.

You might be wondering where are all the inflation is, since the Federal Reserve and other central banks have created so much currency. At this point in time (2019), it appears that inflation has been mostly limited to financial assets (stocks, real estate, etc.), because banks have been the primary recipients of the currency. However, inflation has also been sharply seen in the cost of healthcare, education, and automobiles. If that inflation seeps out into daily consumer goods like food and energy, watch out!

DEFLATION

Countries that are financially distressed also have the option of simply not paying their debts. When countries, states, municipalities, corporations, or individuals are unwilling or unable to pay their debts, debt is effectively "destroyed." Failure to pay debt causes a chain reaction of debt defaults. This canceling of debt also tends to make cash more valuable, thereby increasing the burden of remaining debt. When governments, businesses, and people have less to spend, they tend to pull back, which causes even more economic hardship, including unemployment. This viscous cycle is known as deflation, which wreaked havoc in the 1930s Great Depression (the term hyperdeflation is rarely used).

Whether a country defaults on its debts (causing a deflationary depression) or hyperinflates their currency in order to pay their debts (e.g. Weimar Germany, Venezuela), either scenario wreaks havoc on a country's economy and asset values. In a hyperinflation, local stock markets typically rise, but lose significant value when currency debasement is factored in. As well, nominal asset values might rise (price of homes, etc.) along with general prices, but lose real value.

LAYERS OF COUNTERPARTY RISK

Most people view their savings or checking account as "cash in the bank." But this is absolutely not the case. Sure, today you can go and make a withdrawal and the bank gives you cash. But in reality, when you deposit your currency, you are giving the bank a loan. The bank then takes your money and either loans it out or otherwise invests it.

The bank is only required to keep a fraction of deposits in its reserves. This is called "fractional reserve banking." As a result, banks have little currency in their reserves, and are vulnerable to bank runs (where depositors rapidly withdraw their currency). These risks are compounded when banks make risky investments (think 2008).

So, if a bank becomes insolvent (unable to pay its obligations), you become an unsecured creditor of the bank. In the U.S., the FDIC insures against this risk up to certain dollar amounts. But in a systemic crash, the FDIC would also become insolvent.

A desperate government may conduct a "bail in" for its banks which means that account holders automatically have their funds reduced by a certain percentage. This happened in Cyprus in 2013. In Greece in 2015, the government limited the amount of daily bank withdrawals. This is an example of a capital control, which is meant to keep money in a country, when investors want to take it out.

Stock brokerages also bring with them counterparty risk. If your stocks, bonds, and other financial instruments are held by a brokerage, you don't technically own them. You become a creditor of the brokerage. So, if your brokerage is insolvent, you may not get your assets back in full.

Mutual funds and exchange traded funds (ETFs) also carry this same counterparty risk. You own a share of the mutual fund or the ETF, not the actual shares held within the mutual fund or ETF. So, if you own mutual funds or ETFs through a brokerage, there are two layers of counterparty risk between you and your financial instrument. All of these things: cash, banks, mutual funds, ETFs and brokerages all seem so rock solid, but in reality, they each bear some level of counterparty risk. And worse yet, in a major economic meltdown, institutions and assets with counterparty risk tend to fall like dominos.

DO YOU SEE THE SIGNS?

> *I think we are not on a sustainable fiscal path.* —Jerome Powell, Federal Reserve Chairman (when pressed to comment about the fast-rising national debt in a congressional hearing on February 27, 2018)[90]

You may be thinking, why all the doom and gloom? Well, first off, the Bible warns us to prepare for disaster by diversifying (see Chapter 12). Why would the Bible do that? I think it is because disasters routinely happen. Some are big, some are small, and some are in between. Some are enormous, and we never can know until it is too late.[91]

> *[Jesus] replied, "When evening comes, you say, 'It will be fair weather, for the sky is red,' and in the morning, 'Today it will be stormy, for the sky is red and overcast.' You know how to interpret the appearance of the sky, but you cannot interpret the signs of the times.* (Matthew 16:2-3)

Second, can't you see the storm clouds? Jesus chastised the Pharisees for not recognizing his coming. He likened his coming to predicting the weather on a given day. He was basically saying: "With all of the signs, can't you see that I am the Messiah?" Of course, it wasn't completely obvious, but the signs were there. I suppose when something is a long time in coming, it is very hard to believe it when it finally does come.

The risks to the global financial system are not linear, but rather exponential.[92] In my opinion, it is very easy to underestimate the fragility of our financial system and the speed at which it can seize up. All of the vast debt, unfunded liabilities, currency creation and extreme leverage (margin investing and derivatives) have created a very unstable situation. Our level of diversification should mirror that reality.

DON'T PANIC! TAKE A SENSIBLE APPROACH.

What if I told you that you were going to go on a 1,000-mile-per-hour amusement park ride, but you wouldn't fly off it, because of a super-strong restraint that would keep you in place? Don't panic, but you're on it right now! You are currently moving at about 1,000 miles per hour relative to the center of the earth (due to the earth's spin) and a tremendous downward force called gravity is keeping you from flying into space! Learning about what is really going on in the global economy can also be very frightening and disorienting, but you've been in it your whole life and it's gotten you this far.

There is so much wrong with today's global financial picture and there are numerous facts to support that conclusion. Yet, the world economy is too complex and the interplay of its events too unpredictable to draw any definitive conclusions about how, when, or if it will collapse. Therefore, even if you are aware of impending financial disasters, you still should be measured about how you position your life and finances.

You still need to "prepare" for the status quo. You need to prosper as the global economy continues as is, spending only a moderate amount of time and money insuring against potential catastrophic outcomes. Don't stop making financial and other mainstream investments. You could lose tons of money waiting for a disaster that never comes or is a very long-time in coming. That would be foolish. However, it would be equally foolish not to insure yourself against potential disasters.[93]

WAYS TO DIVERSIFY AGAINST COUNTERPARTY RISK

You don't have to completely believe major economic trouble is coming in order to prepare for it. You only have to believe there is a small possibility it is coming. It's just like fire insurance. Do you think your house is going to burn down in the near future? No, but there is a possibility. In fact, that possibility and many other possibilities are quantified by insurance actuaries, who calculate insurance rates that you can choose to pay (or your lender forces you to pay) for coverages.

As far as I know, there's no insurance company that offers major systemic collapse insurance. If there was such a product, I wouldn't buy it. That's because insurance companies would go down with the sinking ship. However, you can insure against major economic trouble on your own, by owning assets with low or no counterparty risk.

CASH

Okay, I just bashed cash in the paragraphs above, so why am I promoting it now? While it does suffer from inflation, it is very liquid (convertible to other useful assets). Cash or currency is the first flight to safety for investors. If stocks and bonds drop, investors are selling and converting to cash.

Cash is what we think of as money. In all actuality it is currency, legally convertible to nothing. We only accept it because others accept it. A currency is merely a medium of exchange, not an actual store of wealth. And yet, we tend to think of cash in this way, even though it's just fancy paper.

It's good to have some cash in the bank and on some on hand. You need cash to pay bills and buy groceries. Cash in hand (physical bills) is good in case the power is off, credit is offline or banks close. Cash is critical for shifting from one type of investment to another.

GOLD: A BARBAROUS RELIC OR THE ULTIMATE STORE OF WEALTH?

In truth, the gold standard is already a barbarous relic.
—John Maynard Keynes

Many have misquoted the famous economist John Maynard Keynes to have said that "gold is a barbarous relic." It is a horrible misquote, because he was not talking about gold, but rather the specific 1924 gold standard.[94] It has been a long time since any currency in the world has been under a gold standard, which is the ability to convert currency directly into physical gold. A gold standard imposes a strict discipline on currency that bankers and politicians do not favor.

Under the gold standard, a free banking system stands as the protector of an economy's stability and balanced growth... The abandonment of the gold standard made it possible for the welfare statists to use the banking system as a means to an unlimited expansion of credit... In the absence of the gold standard, there is no way to protect savings from confiscation through inflation. —Alan Greenspan, Federal Reserve Chairman 1987-2006[95]

Gold is the ultimate hedge against inflation. Gold has more or less held its purchasing power over the centuries. In other words, a measure of gold (say a troy ounce) would buy approximately the same value of goods today as it did a hundred or a thousand years ago.

Gold is treated as a commodity today, not as money. It played the role of money for thousands of years up until last century. When you look at the currency value of gold it seems volatile. This may seem a little strange, but I prefer to think of the volatility as the currency's volatility and not gold's volatility. Gold is just gold.

Many advisors recommend that 3-10% of investment portfolios should be in precious metals.

Ironically, most people view gold as a risky investment because of its currency price volatility. I submit to you that gold is actually a very stable investment, so stable it's almost boring. It's like my rooftop solar panels. It will take about ten years for me to get a return on my investment and after that I'll make a miniscule daily return (oh yeah—solar panels on your house are a legitimate investment too).

So, why should an investor hold precious metals, when it doesn't earn interest or pay dividends? Well, the reason is that it doesn't suffer inflation or have counterparty risk. It is durable and divisible. Gold and silver just sit there: they don't decay or transform, and they will be there when you might need them. For those reasons, gold and silver are historically the world's preferred stores of wealth.

A quick note on silver. It is historically very similar to gold in its use as money. Therefore, it also carries a very similar investment value. Interestingly, it is also an industrial metal used heavily in electronics. Many believe (based on early-2019 prices), that silver is a better investment than gold because of its relative historical price ratio to gold.[96]

Gold is well known as insurance against systemic risk, war, high inflation, and/or hyperinflation. Many advisors recommend that 3-10% of investment portfolios should be in precious metals. Even the mainstream investment commentator Jim Cramer recommends it and likens it to insurance.[97] Do you have any in your portfolio?

If you really want to protect against counter-party risk, you should buy the physical form of the precious metals (bullion), instead of ETFs like GLD or SLV. As discussed above, these ETFs are subject to counterparty risks. You should also research safe ways to store the bullion.

Precious Metals Practicals:
1. As with anything else, don't overdo it. It is like insurance.
2. If you are buying physical precious metals, be sure not to pay oversized commissions. Shop around.
3. As with other investments, consider buying precious metals in regular, steady increments (e.g. once a month or once a quarter). This is what is called "dollar-cost averaging."

For you doubters out there, consider these questions. If gold isn't important, then why do central banks around the world hoard it? Why has there recently been a rapid increase in central bank holdings? My answer is that it holds value without counterparty risk.

It provides the central banks, and by extension the currencies they represent, with credibility and stability. Ironically, many central bankers, financial leaders and politicians downplay the importance of gold. Gold is the best form of money in existence.[98] When it comes to gold: do as they do, not as they say.

CRYPTOCURRENCIES

> *A cryptocurrency is a digital or virtual currency that uses cryptography for security. A cryptocurrency is difficult to counterfeit because of this security feature. A defining feature of a cryptocurrency, and arguably its most endearing allure, is its organic nature; it is not issued by any central authority, rendering it theoretically immune to government interference or manipulation.* —Investopedia[99]

This new form of currency uses block-chain technology, which is a form of distributed ledger technology that is used in other applications. When applied to currency, it is freed from centralized control and debasement. As of 2019, enormous amounts of money have been invested in cryptocurrencies ("cryptos") like Bitcoin, Ethereum and Ripple. It is evident from the volatility of cryptocurrency prices that much of the investment in them is highly speculative—at least for the time being.

Most cryptos have a fixed number of units that can ever be in existence, which is in great contrast to currencies, which can be "printed" in unlimited amounts. For instance, there will eventually only be 21 million units of Bitcoin (BTC)—never more.[100] In theory, cryptos have no counterparty risk and individual cryptos are protected from inflation. However, like currencies, they are backed by nothing other than public acceptance.

> **Is it possible that we will all be using some form of cryptocurrency instead of our local currencies to buy things in ten or twenty years? Who knows?**

Let me just say that this is a very new type of investment and can be extremely risky. However, I think it could be a legitimate (but small) part of a diversified portfolio if you can emotionally handle its extreme price volatility. Your portfolio would be thanking you if you had bought some Bitcoin in 2012. On the other hand, you might be in great distress if you had bought Bitcoin near one of its extreme highs, only to see your investment crumble.

Be warned that many taxing authorities, including the U.S., treat cryptos like commodities and not currencies. Every time you sell or exchange cryptos, it creates a taxable event, even if you are buying goods. Crypto related taxes become especially tricky when you trade crypto for crypto, which is quite common in the crypto world. In that case, the taxing currency value for each crypto must be determined at that point in time.

Is it possible that we will all be using some form of cryptocurrency instead of our local currencies to buy things in ten or twenty years? Who knows? I suspect that despite the past performance of Bitcoin and other cryptos, the overall currency value of cryptos will tend to slow down as numerous cryptocurrencies are spawned. As a result, cryptos will suffer from inflation and technological challenges. Many inferior cryptos may go to zero (maybe even Bitcoin).

Government regulations may stymie or crush crypto prices. Governments may even adopt their own cryptos as an extension of their national currencies, which could greatly affect the value of other cryptos. Because of these quickly changing dynamics, cryptos may not be a good "buy and hold" type of investment. If you choose to invest in cryptos, be warned of all its hazards and intricacies.

ART AND COLLECTIBLES

Art and other collectibles can also be an effective hedge against counterparty risk and inflation. These types of investments are typically exchanged by the upper echelon of society. If you have the money, why not have an investment where you can also enjoy its artistic value? Be sure to consider the price volatility and liquidity of whatever you intend to purchase.

NO RECOMMENDATION FOR A SPECIFIC ALLOCATION

After explaining many of the concepts in this section to a close friend, he pressed me to recommend a specific asset allocation. I understood his desire to quickly size up his own situation, but I refused to provide him a recommended allocation for many reasons. First and foremost, it is important that each person understand and internalize these concepts and not just superficially apply an allocation.

Second, each person's situation is unique and potentially complex. An allocation doesn't account for income, risk of loss of income, age, health, obligations, personal goals, etc. Robotically applying a formula ignores the less tangible factors that might be the most important factors for that person.

Third, categories of investments such as "stocks" or "real estate" are too vague to be helpful. Some stocks are risky, while some tend to be negatively correlated to the broader market. Some real estate investments are very conservative, while others are highly speculative. So, broad categories within allocations are vague and possibly misleading.

I think I can safely give an example of what to avoid. Here's the portfolio of a couple in their mid-fifties in serious need of diversification:

- $750,000 primary residence (with a $600,000 mortgage loan)
- $50,000 vacation home (with a $25,000 mortgage loan)
- $500,000 in 401(k)/IRA invested in mutual funds (stocks/bonds)
- $20,000 in cash or CD's (i.e. operating/emergency fund)
- $0 in income-generating real estate or other investments
- $0 in alternative investments

What first jumps out is that for a couple in their mid-fifties, they are highly levered in their properties. While the couple has sizeable stock/bond holdings, they are not well protected against a market downturn or high inflation. Their emergency fund is way too small given their mortgage loan amount.

In sum, this couple is heavily relying on the stock and housing markets as they head toward their retirement. If this couple retired thirty years ago, they'd have done well. If they retired near the 2001 and 2008 financial crises, depending on how they handled it, they might not have done well. Hindsight is always 20/20. But, if they retire ten years from now with this type of financial plan, I believe they are taking on significant and unnecessary risk. They still have many years to shift their mutual-fund-heavy portfolio into something diversified and less leveraged.

CONCLUSION

The prudent see danger and take refuge,
  but the simple keep going and pay the penalty.
(Proverbs 22:3)

Whatever your exact view of the world and your local economy is, one must recognize there is always a risk of full or partial systemic collapse. Seriously think through what would happen to your finances if the financial system collapsed; what would you have left?

It's easy to ignore these potentials, much like ignoring the possibility of an infrequent natural disaster, like an earthquake or Tsunami. This is called normalcy bias.

Normalcy bias is a mental state people enter when facing a disaster. It causes people to underestimate both the possibility of a disaster and its possible effects, because it causes people to have a bias to believe that things will always function the way things normally function. This may result in situations where people fail to adequately prepare and, on a larger scale, the failure of governments to include the populace in its disaster preparations.[101]

Everything is okay, until it isn't. The Bible warns us to diversify, so let's do it.

Section IV:

SPIRITUAL INVESTMENTS

Spiritual Investments

If you want a religion to make you feel really comfortable, I certainly don't recommend Christianity.
—C.S. Lewis[102]

If you've read Chapters 1 and 6-10, you've already been sensitized to how important it is to make spiritual investments. Spiritual investments include relationships, time, heart and money. This Section deals with the specifics of spiritual giving and how it affects our lives.

Let's take a minute to indulge in some worldly thinking, but for a spiritual purpose. Imagine being so rich you never have to work again and can indulge yourself daily for the rest of your life. You can travel to exotic locations, engage in expensive hobbies, hire servants, buy gifts for family and friends and literally bathe in cash.

If you are having trouble visualizing this, just go and buy a $2 lottery ticket. Now that the possibility of extreme wealth is real for you, take a few moments to think it through. Just admit it, you've fantasized about this before. You've probably done it many times, maybe even with a spouse or a good friend. I certainly have.

It could be very nice to do all the things you've always wanted to do. All your problems would... still be there!

> *[Very wealthy people in our study] turned out to be a generally dissatisfied lot, whose money has contributed to deep anxieties involving love, work, and family. Indeed, they are frequently dissatisfied even with their sizable fortunes. Most of them still do not consider themselves financially secure; for that, they say, they would require on average one-quarter more wealth than they currently possess.*[103]

The respondents to the study were 120 people with a net worth of $25 million or more. Incredibly, the people surveyed generally did not feel financially secure! They felt they needed to have, on average, another $6.25 million more dollars to be secure. Do you think that if they increased their net worth, they would feel any better?

It's obvious that these people will never feel good about their situation. They have a spiritual problem, one that cannot be solved with more money. Do we, maybe to some degree, have the same problem?

Truly, a person's life is not made up of their possessions or those millionaires would live life with a perma-smile. So, what good is money if you can't feel satisfied with it? Well, as we've learned from the Bible, money isn't for feeling secure. It's for sharing, which can put a smile on your face!

So much good can come from sharing wealth. What good can you do this week by sharing your wealth? If wealth is a just a means to an end, then what is your end? What good do you want to do in the world?

Chapter 15

Motivations for Charitable Giving

Our base natural instinct is to keep everything for ourselves and our families. Also built into our DNA is the desire to share in a way that benefits our immediate community to foster cooperation. But giving to truly spiritual causes or to the needs of people far away takes a measure of faith that goes beyond mere human concerns.

> *Jesus turned and said to Peter, "Get behind me, Satan! You are a stumbling block to me; you do not have in mind the concerns of God, but **merely human concerns**."*
> *Then Jesus said to his disciples, "Whoever wants to be my disciple must deny themselves and take up their cross and follow me. For whoever wants to save their life will lose it, but whoever loses their life for me will find it. What good will it be for someone to gain the whole world, yet forfeit their soul? Or what can anyone give in exchange for their soul? For the Son of Man is going to come in his Father's glory with his angels, and then he will reward each person according to what they have done. (Matthew 16:23-27 emphasis added)*

Jesus calls us to go beyond our natural instinct to save our own souls. We have to be willing to lose our lives to truly follow Jesus. Profoundly, Jesus promises that we will find our eternal life in the process. Not only that, but we will be rewarded in the end. Because our souls go on beyond this lifetime, it matters what we do on earth.

Whatever our basic standard is for honoring God with our wealth, there is a time when we need to move beyond that because of how God has prospered us. It is different for everyone, but God sees our situation and our heart. Jesus beckons us to step out on faith and give *without* seeing an earthly reward.

This kind of giving requires us to have a certain view of the world. We have to be willing to open our eyes and see that there are tremendous needs in the world, both spiritual and physical. Anyone can give token amounts, but to really sacrifice for something, you have to have a sincere belief in the cause.

Sure, people can be socially pressured into giving for a while, but it usually doesn't last. Some might give for a time out of some other ignoble motives. For the most part, truly sacrificial giving takes the healthy spiritual eyes that Jesus described in Matthew 6. Can you see the tremendous needs out there? Can you see how you can make a difference? Do you believe Jesus himself will reward you in his glory and in the presence of his angels?

Here are some biblical motivations for charitable giving.

GOD'S GRACE

> *Praise be to the God and Father of our Lord Jesus Christ, who has blessed us in the heavenly realms with every spiritual blessing in Christ. For he chose us in him before the creation of the world to be holy and blameless in his sight. In love he predestined us for adoption to sonship through Jesus Christ, in accordance with his pleasure and will— to the praise of his glorious grace, which he has freely given us in the One he loves. In him we have redemption through his blood, the forgiveness of sins, in accordance with the riches of God's grace that he lavished on us. (Ephesians 1:3-8)*

God has given us every spiritual blessing we could need. We have faith that our sins are forgiven by the redemption through Jesus' blood. It is a spiritual richness that cannot be repaid through worldly wealth nor any acts of human righteousness. This forms the basis for everything we do, including generous giving. I almost didn't include this motivation because it is so fundamental.

Can the simple knowledge of God's grace alone motivate us to extreme generosity? Can this knowledge push us to the edge of moral perfection? I don't believe so, not for any length of time anyway. God's grace is a catch all concept for spiritual motivation, but it can be hollow without a deeper understanding of what that grace specifically means to us in our lives. Sacrificial giving takes a greater depth of motivation.

FUNDAMENTAL FAIRNESS

> *From everyone who has been given much, much will be demanded; and from the one who has been entrusted with much, much more will be asked.* (Luke 12:48)

One of my favorite qualities of God is his fairness. I suppose you could also call it justness, but that tends to make a person think about crimes and punishments. What I mean by fairness is that God takes everything into account. He knows the complete situation, including people's ability to give.

Take for example people born into poverty in a region with little opportunity. No matter how hard working or clever those people are, the great majority of them will never be able to give as much money as the average person in a first-world region. God would not hold them to the same numerical expectation for giving money. Of course, the opposite is true for many who are reading this book.

He also knows our motives and our hearts. He knows why we do what we do. If we give from impure motives, we do not get a heavenly reward. If we give out of love, we are richly rewarded. He knows exactly how easy or how hard something is for us, even on an emotional and psychological level, and he rewards us accordingly.

GIVING BACK: RICHNESS TOWARD GOD

When we start to accumulate wealth, we become increasingly secure in a worldly way. When we are comfortable and secure for many years to come, we tend to forget God (see Chapter 8). Jesus sharply warns us against this.

> *Then he said to them, "Watch out! Be on your guard against all kinds of greed; life does not consist in an abundance of possessions."*
> *And he told them this parable: "The ground of a certain rich man yielded an abundant harvest. He thought to himself, 'What shall I do? I have no place to store my crops.'*
> *"Then he said, 'This is what I'll do. I will tear down my barns and build bigger ones, and there I will store my surplus grain. And I'll say to myself, "You have plenty of grain laid up for many years. Take life easy; eat, drink and be merry."'*
> *"But God said to him, 'You fool! This very night your life will be demanded from you. Then who will get what you have prepared for yourself?'*

> *"This is how it will be with whoever stores up things for themselves but is not rich toward God."* (Luke 12:15-21)

Are we rich toward God? I think the first area to check is your heart and whether you really give credit to God for what you've accumulated. That is not say you didn't work hard or make great decisions to earn it (unless you inherited it or got it in another easy way). However you got it, God allowed you to have it. Believe it!

> *For by the grace given me I say to every one of you: Do not **think of yourself more highly than you ought, but rather think of yourself with sober judgment, in accordance with the faith God has distributed to each of you.** For just as each of us has one body with many members, and these members do not all have the same function, so in Christ we, though many, form one body, and each member belongs to all the others. We have different gifts, according to the grace given to each of us. If your gift is prophesying, then prophesy in accordance with your faith; if it is serving, then serve; if it is teaching, then teach; if it is to encourage, then give encouragement; **if it is giving, then give generously;** if it is to lead, do it diligently; if it is to show mercy, do it cheerfully.*
> (Romans 12:3-8 emphasis added)

You may wonder if you have the gift of giving. Frankly, I'm not sure if it refers to having a natural heart for giving to others, or if it refers to simply having money (or other resources). Whether you are predisposed to sharing or holding back, we are all called to grow in our faith. Pray that God gives you a generous heart, filled with joy and purpose.

My personal conviction is that if you don't share what you've been given, then you are not rich toward God. Mere token giving mixed with warm fuzzies doesn't cut it. The litmus test is sacrificial giving. If God has given you a lot, he expects you to share it![104]

REWARD IN HEAVEN

> *Do not be overawed when others grow rich,*
>   *when the splendor of their houses increases;*
> *for they will take nothing with them when they die,*

> *their splendor will not descend with them.*
> *Though while they live they count themselves blessed—*
> *and people praise you when you prosper—*
> *they will join those who have gone before them,*
> *who will never again see the light of life.*
> *People who have wealth but lack understanding*
> *are like the beasts that perish.* (Psalm 49:16-20)

Part of me feels bad hitting you, the reader, with this barrage of intense Scriptures. But as I read them, I see that we need their sobering intensity to work against the powerful effects of wealth. Truly, you can't take it with you, and we need to be reminded of what really matters. Even *"counting [yourself as] blessed"* (some form of gratitude) is scorned by God, when not accompanied by understanding and godliness. What you can do, however, is take some of that dangerous wealth and convert it into reward in heaven. It's the safest, most long-term investment out there.

> *Command those who are rich in this present world not to be arrogant nor to put their hope in wealth, which is so uncertain, but to put their hope in God, who richly provides us with everything for our enjoyment. Command them to do good, to be rich in good deeds, and to be generous and willing to share. In this way they will lay up treasure for themselves as a firm foundation for the coming age, so that they may take hold of the life that is truly life.* (1 Timothy 6:17-19)

Imagine your church leader meets with you and says, "I've noticed you are really into your money and come across as arrogant. You're not known in the church for your generosity. You need to step up your good deeds, generosity and sharing your wealth for the sake of your soul!" Whoa! If you didn't have a very good relationship with that leader and a lot of humility, the conversation probably wouldn't go well.

Perhaps your church leader does want to challenge you but is afraid because you intimidate him or her. Perhaps your church leader is afraid you'll stop giving altogether. As a wealthy person in a church, this just isn't the kind of dynamic you want to have. It does no good for anyone. If you are wealthy, set an example of generosity in your church and community, starting with honoring God with generous baseline giving and giving to the needs of the poor.

We need to have people, preferably peers, who can talk to us about sensitive topics like this. These should be people you respect and trust—who you will actually be willing to take input from. Who knows about your wealth situation? Who have you told? If you have serious wealth and have no one to talk to, I urge you to find someone (or better yet, many people) to confide in.

> *"Rejoice in that day and leap for joy, because great is your reward in heaven. For that is how their ancestors treated the prophets.*
>
> *But woe to you who are rich,*
> *   for you have already received your comfort.*
> *Woe to you who are well fed now,*
> *   for you will go hungry.*
> *Woe to you who laugh now,*
> *   for you will mourn and weep.*
> *Woe to you when everyone speaks well of you,*
> *   for that is how their ancestors treated the false prophets.* (Luke 6:23-26)

If you are a church leader, I challenge you to figure out a way to meet the spiritual needs of the wealthy in your church in a way that they can trust. Your relationship with the wealthy person needs to be genuine, with faith, and without envy. You may need to enlist the help of other well-off members of your church who are doing well with their generosity. Even though a wealthy person appears to have everything, he or she can be suffering spiritually because no one is stepping up to talk to them about their spiritual needs—which can be different from the average person.

ACHIEVING A BALANCE THROUGH GIVING

At the risk of being redundant, I wanted to explore the idea of balance again with this famous saying of Agur. After looking at the dangers of wealth, the words make so much sense:

> *"Two things I ask of you, LORD;*
> *   do not refuse me before I die:*
> *Keep falsehood and lies far from me;*

> *give me neither poverty nor riches,*
> *but give me only my daily bread.*
> *Otherwise, I may have too much and disown you*
> *and say, 'Who is the LORD?'*
> *Or I may become poor and steal,*
> *and so dishonor the name of my God.* (Proverbs 30:7-9)

Some of us have so much wealth that we need to give a lot of it away just to keep from being corrupted by it. Even many of the wealthiest people in the world have decided to give away the majority of their fortunes in The Giving Pledge (perhaps even without God as their motivation).[105] I believe using giving as a shield against greed is wise, noble and commendable. It is a great tool to keep the idolatry of mammon in check and to keep your heart close to God!

Chapter 16

Giving More

*Some people are always greedy for more,
but the godly love to give!* (Proverbs 21:26 NLT)

The moment anyone suggests that I need to do more of something, I get defensive. I start thinking about the ways that I have already done enough and what a burden it would be to do more. My pride lashes out and I cling to the idea that I have been righteous and how dare someone call me to do more! I may even question the motives of the person or organization calling me to do more. In a split second, I'm forced to examine my faith, my spiritual condition and my heart.

Attitude is everything, isn't it? Even if we honor God with our wealth, we can still hold back our hearts from wanting to give more. We're afraid we might give up too much. We don't want to lose control of our situation. Deep down, we're afraid Jesus might call us to sell everything we have, like the rich young ruler.

SHOULD WE GIVE AWAY EVERYTHING?

Let me put you at ease. I'm not advocating we give away all our money or sell all of our possessions. Nor do I think the Bible calls us to do so. There, I said it. We already know from the New Testament that many Christians had homes and that some were wealthy. Let me, in the next two paragraphs, address some other examples.

> **I'm not advocating we give away all our money or sell all of our possessions. Nor do I think the Bible calls us to do so.**

Yes, Jesus in his last three years of life essentially lived without his own possessions; but he knew he wouldn't need them! He lived on the goodwill of those with possessions during his travels. Let me restate: Jesus' ministry relied on believers with homes, food, money and other possessions. There's nothing wrong with that arrangement! Jesus even provided for his mother by having her stay with the apostle John: *"From that time on, this disciple took her into his home."* (John 19:27). Good thing John had a home.

Yes, at the beginning of the church, the disciples had terrific hearts and *"sold property and possessions to give to anyone who had need."* (Acts 2:45). The Bible does not say they sold all their property and possessions. Moreover, it was a special situation where numerous converts stayed in Jerusalem much longer than they had planned. The local converts rose to the occasion and met the immediate need. Notably, many of these same Christians were likely receiving aid from their gentile brothers and sisters many years later (collected by the apostle Paul as referenced in 2 Corinthians 8).

Personally, I've never known anyone who has given away all their possessions and money and I've known a lot of godly people. If someone does that, who will take care of them? I don't think anyone should destabilize themselves financially in order to be charitable. What I am really addressing in this chapter isn't necessarily giving in greater amounts, it is learning to love giving!

THE MINDSET OF GIVING MORE

For me, it has taken many years of sacrificial giving to even get to the point where I considered the idea of desiring to give. For so long, I gave only out of duty, faith and honor and didn't think much about my motives for giving. I think it really started to hit me after I had a family. When I started considering the plight of the poor and all that God has given me, I started to naturally feel like I wanted to give.

Now, I look forward to giving to the needy. I don't need anyone to tell me to do it. I don't need to hear a plea at church to prompt me to do it (although that could encourage me to give more). Most of the time, I no longer see giving more as a burden, but rather an opportunity.[106] I want to earn more—so I can give more. I want to control my spending—so I can give more. I want my investments to do well—so I can give more. It's a very different mindset that gives me a sense of satisfaction and builds my faith.

My family and I have a long way to go to have a heart like Jesus, but I want to make that journey. I know deep down that is true for all of us. Some of us might need to see poverty close up to awaken our conscience. Some of us might need to feel the joy of helping others in a direct way. Some might need the spark of seeing a thriving new church, funded by our missions' donations. Get inspired and just do it. Some godly inspiration can go a long way.

WHEN SHOULD I GIVE MORE?

> *I am not commanding you, but I want to test the sincerity of your love by comparing it with the earnestness of others. For you know the grace of our Lord Jesus Christ, that though he was rich, yet for your sake he became poor, so that you through his poverty might become rich.*
> *And here is my judgment about what is best for you in this matter. Last year you were the first not only to give but also to have the desire to do so. Now finish the work, so that your eager willingness to do it may be matched by your completion of it, according to your means. For if the willingness is there, the gift is acceptable according to what one has, not according to what one does not have.* (2 Corinthians 8:8-12)

In context, Paul was using the incredibly generous gift of the Macedonian churches as an example to the Corinthian church. This was a special collection for the impoverished disciples in Judea. The offering was not what the Macedonian or Corinthian churches used to pay their local leaders or to meet local needs, but they saved up and gave, nonetheless.

There are so many far-off needs and, often, they are the greatest needs. Your money can stretch a long way in very impoverished regions. Regardless of whether you give to local or worldwide needs, the passage above contains some great guidelines for giving more.

First off, we should never borrow money in order to give. The Scripture says the *"gift is acceptable according to what one has."* He was essentially saying: "I'm not asking you give beyond your means." I'm fairly certain that Paul (and God by extension) would not condone giving on credit. Borrowing money for charitable giving is literally giving beyond our means.

If you are unsure about where you are at with your personal finances, take some time to figure it out before you give beyond your means. I know sometimes we can have a great heart to give and want to do it even if we have to effectively borrow. We need to resist this urge and only give what God has given us at the present time. God will open many more opportunities for you to give when you have the means.

My cousin, who is a C.P.A., did my taxes one year when I was in college and saw that I had given a huge percentage of my income to my church (I didn't have a lot of expenses at the time). He chastised me and advised me that I should save some of the money for the future. I was thinking, "Get behind me Satan!" But, in hindsight, I see I was wrong. I didn't listen to him, but I wish I had! I even once took out extra on a student loan in order to give to world missions. I'm pretty sure in the long run I ended up shortchanging world missions, because I had to pay that debt with interest and had less to give later.

Many people today, especially young people, are saddled with debt and shouldn't give more. Even if you don't borrow more to give, it may be irresponsible to give more. You have to make sure you are making reasonable headway in paying off any bad debt. Personally, I wouldn't give more (beyond honoring God with a percentage of your income) until all my bad debt was gone. I would let my desire to give more drive me to get more serious about trimming down my lifestyle and paying off my bad debt. (See Chapter 3 for a refresher on bad debt).

Secondly, we should give more when we have a genuine desire to do so. The Scripture is filled with words that show a true desire to share. When I say, "give more," I mean **up and above** our baseline offering that we give to honor God. What we give to honor God should be based on our income and given steadfastly, because it is about honoring God and meeting our social responsibility to our church (see Chapter 1).

If you don't have that genuine desire to give more, I recommend holding back, because that might mean you are doing so under some sort of compulsion. Determining whether you genuinely want to give more or not is not always easy, especially if there is a drive or campaign pushing you to give. I don't think peer pressure to do godly things is necessarily a bad thing, but we have to make sure our hearts keep up with whatever is going on around us, or we risk becoming bitter in the long run.

SHOULD WE WAIT UNTIL WE ARE OUT OF ALL DEBT OR FINANCIALLY SET BEFORE WE GIVE MORE?

Being out of all debt would mean you paid off all your bad debt, but that you also paid off all your student, car, home and business debt! That is a wonderful goal and place to be, but most people won't achieve that until they are close to retirement. To follow such an arbitrary rule ignores our net wealth. Many people have debt, but their net worth is in the hundreds of thousands or millions. In my opinion,

Christians whose net worth is in the hundreds of thousands or millions should be generously giving more.

Also, to follow a rule like that would ignore our consumerism. We can always borrow more to buy more and never achieve being out of all debt. We should take a close look at the size of our figurative barns and consider tearing some of them down to build smaller ones! I know that some Christian financial commentators recommend accumulating significant wealth before giving more than a baseline amount. I am not one of them.

> **We should take a close look at the size of our figurative barns and consider tearing some of them down to build smaller ones!**

There are many silos in which to save up: vehicle paid off, home paid off, 401(k)s stuffed and maxed, children's college funds stuffed and maxed, etc. These are all great things to do, but we need to be careful we don't justify our stinginess in the name of being responsible. Even responsible, well-to-do earners are rarely ever able to fill those big silos. We can't wait until everything is perfect in our financial life to start giving generously.

AVOID SELF-RIGHTEOUSNESS IN GIVING

"Be careful not to practice your righteousness in front of others to be seen by them. If you do, you will have no reward from your Father in heaven.

So when you give to the needy, do not announce it with trumpets, as the hypocrites do in the synagogues and on the streets, to be honored by others. Truly I tell you, they have received their reward in full. But when you give to the needy, do not let your left hand know what your right hand is doing, so that your giving may be in secret. Then your Father, who sees what is done in secret, will reward you." (Matthew 6:1-4)

The way Jesus first addresses giving to the needy in his Sermon on the Mount is very curious. If most of us gave a sermon addressing giving to the needy, we would probably highlight the plight of the poor and talk about how important it was that we meet their needs. Instead, Jesus just assumes that we will give to the needy and quickly moves on to addressing our hearts while giving. He deals with our motives for giving, specifically addressing the futility of seeking praise from men. He does the same for prayer and fasting.

Many philanthropists have their names on buildings or have foundations named after them. While it seems appropriate to recognize a large donor, I doubt the recognition has helped their heart or spiritual reward. I suppose it is possible to have a building or charity named after you and you not become self-righteous, but I don't think that was the spirit Jesus taught us to have.

I don't want to discourage anyone from starting a foundation or paying for a church building. In fact, it can be a special way of making a spiritual investment that might not otherwise get accomplished through incremental giving. For instance, you could start a missions society to help start churches in your region. You could create a non-profit to do a specific kind of charity work. Whatever your passion, I encourage you to pray, get advice and examine your motives before proceeding. Don't create a monument to yourself!

Most of us will never have the opportunity to have a building named after us, but there are things we can do that can be tantamount to asking for that sort of honor. It is easy to let money define us, even when giving. I think preserving anonymity in giving is Jesus' key practical advice for us. Also, we can avoid being hypocrites by working on our genuine love for the needy. Let's pray about it, get personally involved and work together with others to meet needs.

Lastly, I want to point out that giving is not a substitute for dealing with sin in our lives.

> *With what shall I come before the LORD*
> *   and bow down before the exalted God?*
> *Shall I come before him with burnt offerings,*
> *   with calves a year old?*
> *Will the LORD be pleased with thousands of rams,*
> *   with ten thousand rivers of olive oil?*
> *Shall I offer my firstborn for my transgression,*
> *   the fruit of my body for the sin of my soul?*
> *He has shown you, O mortal, what is good.*
> *   And what does the LORD require of you?*
> *To act justly and to love mercy*
> *   and to walk humbly with your God.* (Micah 6:6-8)

Being righteous before God is always more important than

giving (sorry Robin Hood)! Good acts on our part do not make up for bad acts or a bad heart. It is easy to fall into this trap and give out of guilt or self-righteousness. Instead, let's let our giving drive us toward personal righteousness.

> *"Woe to you, teachers of the law and Pharisees, you hypocrites! You clean the outside of the cup and dish, but inside they are full of greed and self-indulgence. Blind Pharisee! First clean the inside of the cup and dish, and then the outside also will be clean."* (Matthew 23:25-26)

We tend to want to look good to feel good. Jesus says, stop worrying about how you look on the outside, focus on how you are on the inside. Ouch! Jesus so often directs us to look at and purify our motives. Our giving should be an expression of our righteousness, not a replacement for it.

A GENEROUS, SERVING LIFESTYLE

> *When Jesus came into Peter's house, he saw Peter's mother-in-law lying in bed with a fever. He touched her hand and the fever left her, and she got up and began to wait on him.*
> *When evening came, many who were demon-possessed were brought to him, and he drove out the spirits with a word and healed all the sick.* (Matthew 8:14-16)

Jesus led the way in generosity. Sometimes, he spent most of his day just serving people. In this case, he healed *all* the sick, during the day and in the evening. His heart was to meet the needs around him, and he did it with love and compassion.

> **Jesus led the way in generosity.**

We don't need the gift of healing to be like Jesus. We just need to serve by meeting needs. For those of us with significant wealth, we have the special opportunity to serve in ways others cannot. It doesn't matter if your acts of kindness are random or well-planned.

There are countless ways for any of us can serve others. But here are some ideas for those with significant wealth:

Giving More

1. Purchasing something for someone that they really need
2. Helping a single parent or an elderly person
3. Meeting a special need in the church
4. Sponsoring conference or camp attendance

Chapter 17

Giving to the Poor

If you help the poor, you are lending to the Lord — and he will repay you! (Proverbs 19:17 NLT)

This tiny chapter does not do justice to this subject and it is not meant to. In the context of this book, I am presenting this as one of the options for spiritual investing. Although it is "one of the options," as you'll see below, it really isn't an option. Churches, as the body of Christ, should be like Christ and help the needy—especially those inside the church. As individual Christians, we also have the same responsibility.

There are many books on this subject that are worth reading. In fact, I encourage you to choose one and read it. I recently read the 2017 book *Jesus and the Poor* by Dr. G. Steve Kinnard. He aptly points out that Jesus "spent more time with the poor, the sick, the hurting, the helpless, and the hopeless than any other group within his world."[107]

> *Today, over 20,000 children will die due to conditions of poverty. Today, some 800 million people will go hungry. Today, around 27 million children will serve as slaves in the slave industry. These people are desperate. We don't know their names. We may never see their faces, but they are out there.* —Jesus and the Poor, p.86

The need is staggering and overwhelming. Perhaps part of what you give to your church goes to meeting the needs of the poor, but in this chapter, I am calling you to give more. If you want a heavy-duty comprehensive view on the needs of the poor and first-world charitable giving, read *Rich Christians in an Age of Hunger* by Ronald J. Sider.[108] The title says it all. The next section is a brief reality check from Sider's book and a few other sources.

THE SAD STATE OF CHARITABLE GIVING IN THE UNITED STATES

But isn't the United States the most generous country in the world? Aren't the Christians within it the most generous people on the planet? And isn't that generosity increasing as the U.S. gets wealthier? Sad to say, the answers to those questions are no, no and no. It's time to sober up and humble ourselves.

> *For by the grace given me I say to every one of you: Do not think of yourself more highly than you ought, but rather think of yourself with sober judgment, in accordance with the faith God has distributed to each of you.* (Romans 12:3)

Although the U.S. gives more foreign aid than any other country, based on income it is one of the stingiest.[109] Based on income, the U.S. gives about: half that of France and Germany, a third of the U.K. and Netherlands, and five times less than Norway and Sweden. As far as industrialized countries go, only Italy is stingier. Alarmingly, a twenty-year trend shows that the richer the U.S. gets, the less it shares with others.[110]

> *The average American has grown more tight-fisted in recent years, donating a smaller portion of his or her income to charity than he or she did 10 years ago. In some ways, that shift makes sense following the Great Recession, which slashed personal incomes and wealth. Yet even as the country's economy started to recover, Americans have remained stingier than before, according to new research by economists at Texas A&M University.* —The Atlantic [111]

The average person (not Christian) in the U.S. gives 2.3% of his or her income to charities.[112] Despite the fact that "American Christians are the most affluent single group of Christians in two thousand years of church history," we only do a little better than the general populous. Sider postulates that the typical U.S. Christian gives a combined total of 4.3% of their income to their church and other charities.[113]

Even though disposable incomes in the U.S. have doubled from 1968 to 2011, the per person charitable giving has steadily fallen from 3.11% to 2.32% during that time period.[114] So, what do all these gloomy statistics mean? It means that mammon is winning the war in the "Land of the Free" and I suspect that is true for most other industrialized countries. As followers of Jesus Christ, we are called to a much higher expectation.

ARE WE GOOD SAMARITANS?

> On one occasion an expert in the law stood up to test Jesus. "Teacher," he asked, "what must I do to inherit eternal life?"
> "What is written in the Law?" he replied. "How do you read it?"
> He answered, "'Love the Lord your God with all your heart and with all your soul and with all your strength and with all your mind'; and, 'Love your neighbor as yourself.'"
> You have answered correctly," Jesus replied. "Do this and you will live."
> But he wanted to justify himself, so he asked Jesus, "And who is my neighbor?"
> In reply Jesus said: "A man was going down from Jerusalem to Jericho, when he was attacked by robbers. They stripped him of his clothes, beat him and went away, leaving him half dead. A priest happened to be going down the same road, and when he saw the man, he passed by on the other side. So too, a Levite, when he came to the place and saw him, passed by on the other side. But a Samaritan, as he traveled, came where the man was; and when he saw him, he took pity on him. He went to him and bandaged his wounds, pouring on oil and wine. Then he put the man on his own donkey, brought him to an inn and took care of him. The next day he took out two denarii and gave them to the innkeeper. 'Look after him,' he said, 'and when I return, I will reimburse you for any extra expense you may have.'
> "Which of these three do you think was a neighbor to the man who fell into the hands of robbers?" The expert in the law replied, "The one who had mercy on him." Jesus told him, "Go and do likewise." (Luke 10:25-37)

An "expert in the law" (lawyer) came to evaluate Jesus' doctrinal stance. It seems his testing of Jesus was not hostile, but that he wanted to know how to be right with God. After getting his answer, he realized that he might be falling short on the loving your neighbor part. As any good lawyer would, he demanded to know the exact scope of his obligations. So, he asked another question, *"And who is my neighbor?"* Don't we do the same sort of thing when we read the Bible?

As was so often the case, Jesus took what could have been a trifling, mundane discussion and turned it into a mind-blowing, heart-melting lesson for the person asking (and for all of us reading). Imagine the lesson you might get, if you were able to ask Jesus a question in person? You'd never forget it! Just like the lawyer, we should examine our lives and sincerely ask the question, "Who is my neighbor?"

A close reading of this passage reveals that being a Good Samaritan is more than just a lofty ideal. Jesus expects all of us to meet the physical needs of strangers! The Samaritan, whose religious status was inferior to that of the priest or Levite, was actually the righteous one in God's eyes, because of what he did. Does our religious pedigree stop us from loving our neighbor? Does our service to God in other areas exempt us from meeting physical needs?

Honestly, part of me didn't want to include a discussion of this Scripture because I fall so short of the standard Jesus set! As I write, I am repenting of a lack of being a Good Samaritan. I'm working with others in my church to put together community service group projects. My family decided to put together care packages for the needy we see on the streets. I'm looking into increasing my giving to aid organizations. I don't know how much of a difference my efforts will make, but I want to work at making it part of who I am.

SITUATIONAL AND SHREWD GIVING

Another way to look at the Good Samaritan passage is to say that Jesus expects us to meet the needs of those that are around us. The Samaritan's giving was in the moment, situational. The Samaritan didn't pass by and tell himself, "I'll only give to the needy Samaritan fund, but let the locals take care of this guy." We cannot meet all the needs in the world, but when something presents itself right in front of us, shouldn't we help? We know this is right, because so much of Jesus' ministry involved situational giving.[115]

Notice that the Samaritan was efficient and shrewd in meeting the beaten man's needs. He didn't allow it to derail his business trip. He ensured his payment to the innkeeper wouldn't be wasted by expecting an accounting. I suspect this wasn't the first time the

Samaritan had helped others (even though he is likely a hypothetical character). We should also try to give in an effective and efficient way.

Loving God is loving people. Loving people is loving God. How can we be Christians if we do not love our neighbor? Many of us live in places where most people's basic physical needs are always met. We may go days, weeks, or months without seeing someone in need, but that doesn't mean the needy aren't around us. People in need are often shunned, tucked away and marginalized. As churches and as individuals, we need to seek out the needy and help them.

A MODEL SOCIETY THAT AVOIDED SLAVERY AND HELPED THE POOR

Speak up for those who cannot speak for themselves,
 for the rights of all who are destitute.
Speak up and judge fairly;
 defend the rights of the poor and needy. (Proverbs 31:8-9)

Being poor in most nations three thousand years ago meant you were either a slave or completely destitute. There was no such thing as "human rights." Most people at that time were what we would consider slaves today. These were not model societies. The poor were exploited, despised and discarded. That's just the way people treated each other.

The Israelite society, however, had a social structure designed by the Almighty. He designed the society into tribes and families that held family lands, where each family could provide for itself. There originally was no king that would centralize power into the hands of a few. God provided prophets to administer spiritual leadership without corrupting society. God's word was revolutionary in many ways, because it brought a level of equality and social rights never before seen.

God set up a system of debt forgiveness that would protect families from permanently losing their lands. He made laws against involuntary and generational slavery. He designed a portion of the tithe to be set aside for the needy. Despite all of that, individual Israelites were still confronted with the plight of the poor and needy. Even with all of the money spent on social programs today, the same is true today.

> *If anyone is poor among your fellow Israelites in any of the towns of the land the LORD your God is giving you, do not be hardhearted or tightfisted toward them. Rather, be openhanded and freely lend them whatever they need. Be careful not to harbor this wicked thought: "The seventh year, the year for canceling debts, is near," so that you do not show ill will toward the needy among your fellow Israelites and give them nothing. They may then appeal to the LORD against you, and you will be found guilty of sin. Give generously to them and do so without a grudging heart; then because of this the LORD your God will bless you in all your work and in everything you put your hand to. There will always be poor people in the land. Therefore I command you to be openhanded toward your fellow Israelites who are poor and needy in your land.* (Deuteronomy 15:7-11)

God considered a lack of long-term debt forgiveness a sin. He even considered it wicked not to lend before a debt forgiveness year. Many modern societies have loosely grabbed onto the idea of debt forgiveness and allow individuals to file bankruptcy, though some bankruptcy protections have been curtailed in recent times (at least in the U.S.). However, the reality is that our societies are more or less designed to turn people into debt slaves.

Alright, I'll get off the political soapbox. Whatever the situation is in your country or region, the issue of providing for the needy is not a political one—at least as far as God is concerned. Even in a well-designed society, people's hearts are easily corrupted, which in turn corrupts the system. The Israelites often disobeyed God and the model society God set up would often become dysfunctional. Injustice would take over and poverty would increase.

God knows that we will always have the needy. You might even conclude from the Scriptures that it is a permanently unsolvable problem (see Matthew 26:11, Mark 14:7, or John 12:8). God didn't frame the issue in terms of finding a societal solution, but rather as a test of our love and compassion. God commanded individual generosity and promised to reward it. Though we do not have a theocracy to coordinate efforts, we have churches and other organizations that can help support the poor and needy.

GOD SEES OUR COMPASSION AND REWARDS US

> *Blessed are those who have regard for the weak;*
> *the LORD delivers them in times of trouble.*
> *The LORD protects and preserves them—*
> *they are counted among the blessed in the land—*
> *he does not give them over to the desire of their foes.*
> *The LORD sustains them on their sickbed*
> *and restores them from their bed of illness.*
> (Psalm 41:1-3)[116]

I love this passage, because it shows us that God recognizes our compassion and rewards us for it. God is compassionate and loves to see that same quality in us. While much of our reward lies in heaven, God dispenses some of it on earth as well. It never hurts to build up some godly karma. Conversely,

> *Whoever shuts their ears to the cry of the poor*
> *will also cry out and not be answered.*
> (Proverbs 21:13)

Over the years, pop artists have produced songs and organized concerts that have brought attention and support for the poor. Who can forget 1985's *We Are The World?*[117] From time to time, I still hear Phil Collins's catchy song, *Another Day In Paradise.*[118] The most moving to me is George Michael's *Praying for Time.*[119] I especially like the lyrics because it really hits on some of the core issues that hold us back from giving. If you need some inspiration, go online and listen to these songs!

QUICK PRACTICALS FOR GIVING TO THE POOR

> *"Look, Lord! Here and now I give half of my possessions to the poor..."* (Luke 19:8 Zacchaeus speaking to Jesus)

> *She opens her arms to the poor and extends her hands to the needy.* (Proverbs 31:20)

1. Get into the habit of giving to the poor and needy. Like any other type of giving, it takes practice and grows on you.
2. Feel great about sharing your wealth! God does!
3. Where possible, give anonymously, in order to maximize your reward in heaven.
4. Give to organizations that actually serve the poor (look carefully at what they actually do).
5. Give to efficient organizations that have low administrative cost ratios.
6. Participate in or conduct a fundraiser. Get others, including corporate donors involved.
7. Be hands on with your giving! Go to the soup kitchen and serve. After giving to people on the street, look them in the eye and shake hands with them. Invite them to church. If you have time, talk with them. Be creative and figure out ways to serve people locally. If you see a situational need, don't be afraid to help meet it!

Chapter 18

Evangelism & Missions

> Then Jesus came to them and said, "All authority in heaven and on earth has been given to me. Therefore go and make disciples of all nations, baptizing them in the name of the Father and of the Son and of the Holy Spirit, and teaching them to obey everything I have commanded you. And surely I am with you always, to the very end of the age." (Matthew 28:18-20)

Jesus' plan was not the military conquest his countrymen had hoped for. Instead of physically liberating Judea, he spiritually liberated souls around the world. The same battle for souls' rages today. What greater calling is there? What could be more important than bringing the good news that brings eternal salvation to all nations?

Jesus' plan cannot be accomplished cheaply, because his teachings require person to person involvement in *"teaching them to obey everything I have commanded you."* The apostles required three years of daily, in-person training. How much training do we need? When reading the New Testament, you can't go far without seeing all the *"one another"* commands and numerous examples of deep personal involvement amongst the believers. It is no different today.

> Jesus went through all the towns and villages, teaching in their synagogues, proclaiming the good news of the kingdom and healing every disease and sickness. When he saw the crowds, he had compassion on them, because they were harassed and helpless, like sheep without a shepherd. Then he said to his disciples, "The harvest is plentiful but the workers are few. Ask the Lord of the harvest, therefore, to send out workers into his harvest field." (Matthew 9:35-38)

The world cannot be won for Jesus through television ads or the internet. It takes workers. Syndicated preaching cannot replace the personal interaction needed to help us grow in Christ. Each community and each person needs to have the gospel preached to them in a way that they can relate to (1 Corinthians 9:19-23). Jesus needs you to take up this work in your community and, if you can help, to financially contribute to missions work around the world.

PUT YOUR MONEY WHERE YOUR MOUTH IS: SUPPORTING THOSE WHO PREACH THE GOSPEL

> *How, then, can they call on the one they have not believed in? And how can they believe in the one of whom they have not heard?* ***And how can they hear without someone preaching to them?*** *And how can anyone preach unless they are sent? As it is written: "How beautiful are the feet of those who bring good news!"* (Romans 10:14-15 emphasis added)

While opening your mouth is free, there are many aspects of spreading the gospel that are not. Paying minister's salaries and paying for church facilities is not cheap. Funding or being a part of missions work takes great faith and financial sacrifice. If we really believe in the Great Commission, then we must also believe in being generous towards missions work.

We know that *"the Lord has commanded that those who preach the gospel should receive their living from the gospel."* (1 Corinthians 9:14). If money is well managed and preachers have integrity in their work, financial support can increase the spread of the gospel. Even Jesus relied on financial support.

> *After this, Jesus traveled about from one town and village to another, proclaiming the good news of the kingdom of God. The Twelve were with him, and also some women who had been cured of evil spirits and diseases: Mary (called Magdalene) from whom seven demons had come out; Joanna the wife of Chuza, the manager of Herod's household; Susanna; and many others. These women were helping to support them out of their own means.* (Luke 8:1-3)

Early in Jesus' ministry, he sent the apostles out to preach and he instructed them to rely on the support of their listeners (Matthew

10:5-15). The apostle Paul also relied on support from churches to conduct his missionary work.

> *Was it a sin for me to lower myself in order to elevate you by preaching the gospel of God to you free of charge? I robbed other churches by receiving support from them so as to serve you. And when I was with you and needed something, I was not a burden to anyone, for the brothers who came from Macedonia supplied what I needed.*
> (2 Corinthians 11:7-9)

Although he could support himself as a part-time tentmaker, Paul was able to devote himself full-time to preaching and teaching whenever he received enough support from the churches. In some cases, giving from churches made up for a lack of giving in other churches. Paul also received support from individuals like Phoebe.

> *I commend to you our sister Phoebe, a deacon of the church in Cenchreae. I ask you to receive her in the Lord in a way worthy of his people and to give her any help she may need from you, for she has been the benefactor of many people, including me.* (Romans 16:1-2)

As you can see below, the Philippian church was greatly commended for their support of Paul's ministry.

> *Yet it was good of you to share in my troubles. Moreover, as you Philippians know, in the early days of your acquaintance with the gospel, when I set out from Macedonia, not one church shared with me in the matter of giving and receiving, except you only; for even when I was in Thessalonica, you sent me aid more than once when I was in need. Not that I desire your gifts; what I desire is that more be credited to your account. I have received full payment and have more than enough. I am amply supplied, now that I have received from Epaphroditus the gifts you sent. They are a fragrant offering, an acceptable sacrifice, pleasing to God. And my God will meet all your needs according to the riches of his glory in Christ Jesus.* (Philippians 4:14-20)

Most of the influence that the gospel has had in the world today can be traced back to Paul's missionary journeys and the generosity of the early believers. Truly, they fulfilled Jesus' command to make disciples of all nations by their devotion, faith and financial sacrifice! I doubt the early disciples in Macedonia or Phillipi could have imagined the lasting impact their contributions made.

> Most of the influence that the gospel has had in the world today can be traced back to Paul's missionary journeys and the generosity of the early believers.

There are many places in the world today that need the gospel. Someone has to go. Could it be you? Of course, our own communities are a mission field that need workers. We may never go on a missionary journey, but we can still participate in world evangelism. We can pray. We can give. For every person that goes, many more have to stay and give.

Here are some specific ideas related to giving more for evangelism:

1. Up the percentage of your income that you give to your church. This will provide for the needs and growth of your local congregation.
2. Give specifically for world missions. Your church may organize this, or you might have opportunity to give funds directly.
3. Rather than simply giving more, you could peg your extra giving to funds raised through overtime or side jobs. This might give you more satisfaction and motivation, because you are giving that specific time for supporting evangelism.
4. Set aside a portion of funds you receive from an inheritance, sizeable bonus, or similar event for supporting evangelism.

INVESTING IN YOUR OWN FELLOWSHIP AND EVANGELISM

Anyone who can communicate, can tell someone else about Jesus. In very rare cases, that's all it takes. But the great majority of the time, helping someone accept the gospel takes an investment of love, hospitality, time and resources (see 1 Thessalonians 2:7-12). The saving gospel may be free, but the delivery of it is not. The same goes for fellowship in the church.

If you've reached out to others, you know the effort and resources it takes. You've had people over and fed them. You've gone out to eat. You've pitched in for events. You've given out bibles (although now anyone with a smart phone can read the Bible without extra cost). These are things we should all be eager to do.

But if you have significant wealth, you are in a great position to take this type of spiritual investing to the next level. How about covering the check at a restaurant, even if it is a large group? What about funding an entire event? You could pay for others to attend a retreat, seminar, or summer camp. The sky's the limit and the great thing is that you would be able see the impact in your local congregation. Of course, these gifts could be anonymous where appropriate.

It might seem a little awkward to use money so directly to influence fellowship and personal evangelism. Of course, we cannot buy ourselves a spiritual relationship or pay people to follow Jesus. However, a little generosity can really make an impact. The idea should not come as a shock to us. See the following Parable of the Shrewd Manager or Unjust Steward, depending on your bible translation.

> *Jesus told his disciples: "There was a rich man whose manager was accused of wasting his possessions. So he called him in and asked him, 'What is this I hear about you? Give an account of your management, because you cannot be manager any longer.'*
>
> *"The manager said to himself, 'What shall I do now? My master is taking away my job. I'm not strong enough to dig, and I'm ashamed to beg— I know what I'll do so that, when I lose my job here, people will welcome me into their houses.'*
>
> *"So he called in each one of his master's debtors. He asked the first, 'How much do you owe my master?'*
>
> *"'Nine hundred gallons of olive oil,' he replied.*
>
> *"The manager told him, 'Take your bill, sit down quickly, and make it four hundred and fifty.'*
>
> *"Then he asked the second, 'And how much do you owe?'*
>
> *"'A thousand bushels of wheat,' he replied.*
>
> *"He told him, 'Take your bill and make it eight hundred.'*
>
> *"The master commended the dishonest manager because he had acted shrewdly. For the people of this world are more shrewd in dealing with their own kind than are the people of the light. I tell you, use worldly wealth to gain friends for yourselves, so that when it is gone, you will be*

welcomed into eternal dwellings.

"Whoever can be trusted with very little can also be trusted with much, and whoever is dishonest with very little will also be dishonest with much. So if you have not been trustworthy in handling worldly wealth, who will trust you with true riches? And if you have not been trustworthy with someone else's property, who will give you property of your own?

"No one can serve two masters. Either you will hate the one and love the other, or you will be devoted to the one and despise the other. You cannot serve both God and money."

The Pharisees, who loved money, heard all this and were sneering at Jesus. He said to them, "You are the ones who justify yourselves in the eyes of others, but God knows your hearts. What people value highly is detestable in God's sight. (Luke 16:1-15)

Who are these friends we are supposed to gain for ourselves? Why will that cause us to be welcomed into eternal dwellings? Honestly, I think this is one of the most difficult parables to understand, because of the dishonest acts of the manager. I believe this passage is talking about using our wealth for fellowship and evangelism. I don't completely understand the meaning of this passage, but I really like this interpretation:

> Jesus' parable of the unjust manager is one of the most striking in all the Gospels. Obviously, it would be pressing the parable beyond the point of comparison to interpret it as an endorsement of dishonest business practices. Jesus' point is simply to show us what money is really for. Typically we think of ourselves first when we answer that question. But Jesus invites us to realize that, first, our money isn't really ours -- we're simply managing it for its real owner, God. Second, even "filthy lucre" can be pressed into the service of God and our neighbor. When it is, the benefits will last beyond this life -- which the things we buy for ourselves won't. For example, money can be used to spread the gospel, through which the Holy Spirit will gather believers into Christ's church. We will enjoy blessed fellowship with these believers forever, long after the money itself is gone.[120]

GENEROSITY MAKES THE CHURCH SHINE

You are the light of the world. A town built on a hill cannot be hidden. Neither do people light a lamp and put it under a bowl. Instead they put it on its stand, and it gives light to everyone in the house. In the same way, let your light shine before others, that they may see your good deeds and glorify your Father in heaven. (Matthew 5:14-16)

What sort of good deeds make others glorify God? What really makes our light shine? Many things can impact individuals around us like having firm convictions, biblical wisdom, tight-knit relationships and a Christ-like attitude. On a church-wide level, however, these contrasts to the world-at-large can be perceived as extreme, threatening, and weird. Such is the burden of truly following Jesus (John 15:18-25, 2 Timothy 3:1-13).

And yet there are many reasons for the world to be attracted to true Christians and their fellowship. When connected with God, we are transformed into honest, hard-working, law-abiding, loving people. Certainly, having a Christ-like love for each other makes the church shine brightly (John 13:34-35). But in our modern culture, our love is very often limited to just our social interactions.

A missing ingredient in many fellowships is love in the form of physical service to one another. As well, we can fail to serve the community-at-large. I believe that an important part of our heart and passion are suppressed when we do not love fully as Jesus did. People want to be in church where they feel taken care of. People also want to be in a church that serves!

When the church first started, the new disciples had a sincere and complete love, which included meeting each other's physical needs. The bible records that they "enjoy[ed] the favor of all the people. And the Lord added to their number daily those who were being saved. (Acts 2:47)." Even the religious leaders who had killed Jesus were stymied in their persecution of the apostles, because of their good deeds (Acts 4:1-22).

Generosity, charity and service cannot be hidden under a bowl. When a church takes care of its needy members and its local community, it is respected both inside and outside the church (Acts 2:44-47, Acts 5:12-16, Acts 6:1-7, Galatians 6:10; no freeloading though, see 2 Thessalonians 3:10).[121] When a church serves the community around it, it is honored and revered.

> *"For where your treasure is, there your heart will be also. The eye is the lamp of the body. If your eyes are healthy, your whole body will be full of light. But if your eyes are unhealthy, your whole body will be full of darkness. If then the light within you is darkness, how great is that darkness!"* (Matthew 6:21-23)

Remember this passage? What applies to individuals also applies to individual churches. Is your church a generous church with light in its eyes? Is your church the town built on the hill that shines brightly? If you really want to see your church grow, generosity may be what jump-starts or supercharges that growth.

IS IT TIME FOR GREAT WORKS?

Isn't time the real currency we are spending every day? If money isn't a problem for us, then we can purchase, in a sense, the precious commodity of time. But time to do what?

Rather than continuing to focus on making and giving money, you might be in a better position to serve with your time. If you're thinking about retiring from your career or business, then consider pursuing great works like these:

1. Leadership roles
2. Community service projects
3. Missions work
4. Starting a new ministry to meet a specific need
5. Serving the church in areas like children's ministry, building duties, ushering, etc.

Final Thoughts

There are many other ways to invest or give, more than I could ever possibly write about. This book is merely a guide; but remember that the Scriptures you read are truth. It is ultimately your choice what you do with the wealth that God has blessed you with. I sincerely hope that you use it in way that truly benefits you, your family and those around you.

Whatever your situation: young and starting out, in debt, breaking even, or wealthy, what matters is the direction you are going in. Wherever you are, have faith, apply the Scriptures and be inspired for your future. If you let God shape you, you'll become wise in this age, paving your way for the age to come.

What is it in your heart that you would like to do? Talk to someone you trust about your vision and how you want to get there. Ultimately, we all need to work out our own salvation with fear and trembling, balancing our needs and our physical family's needs with giving to others.

Consumerism is an idol that Christians are in danger of being seduced by. It competes to become the story within which we live our lives. —Craig Bartholomew[122]

I started the book by asking you about the vision you had for your life. I asked, "What is the story in which you will live your life?" Is it a story of financial discipline, a healthy perspective about money, wealth growth, and godly generosity? You decide. Will God say this to you on that day?

Well done, good and faithful servant! You have been faithful with a few things; I will put you in charge of many things. Come and share your master's happiness!
(Matthew 25:21)

I'll see you on the other side.

Topical Index

401(k) (of the IRS Code): 31, 48, 62, 69, 113, 118, 121, 122, 148, 164.
529 plans—Internal Revenue Code 26 U.S.C. §529: 122-123.

A

Advertising: 36.
Advice: 4, 6, 33, 45, 71, 95, 102-103, 112, 126, 129-130, 137, 165.
Alternative investments: 138, 148.
Anger: 17.
Approval/disapproval (of God): 17, 85.
Arrogance: 61, 76.
Asset allocation: 148.
Attribution bias/self-serving bias: 69, 82-83, 86, 112, 149.

B

Bad debt: 15, 44-45, 50, 54, 57, 77, 122, 163.
Bankruptcy: 43, 92, 118, 173.
Bitcoin: 146-147.
Bonds: 108, 113, 115, 118, 120-121, 132, 138, 141, 144, 148.
Borrowing: 48, 56, 121, 140, 162.
Budget: 29, 35, 37, 50, 140.
Business: 6, 28, 33, 69-70, 75, 78, 88, 90, 102, 106, 112-113, 115, 119, 125, 132, 133-134, 140, 163, 171, 181, 183.

C

Cash: 38, 48, 102, 106-108, 115, 118, 121, 132, 135, 139, 140-142, 144, 148, 151.
Capital appreciation: 115, 118, 130.
CDs: 120-121.
Charity: 165, 169, 182.
Cheerful giving: 31.
Church: 6-7, 10, 17-22, 25-32, 39, 42, 49, 62, 66, 74, 88-89, 128, 157-158, 161-163, 165, 167-169, 171-173, 175, 177-179, 181-183, 185, 191-192, 199, 200.
College: 10, 38, 46, 92, 124-126, 162-164.
Compulsion: 20-21, 30-31, 33, 163.
Confidence: 14, 125.
Consumer debt: 14, 44.
Consumerism: 74, 164, 184.
Contentment: 37, 73, 97.
Corporations: 38, 114, 140.
Cosigning loans: 43.
Coverdell education savings accounts: 122-123.

Counterparty risk: 138-139, 144-148.
Credit cards: 50.
Cryptocurrency: 146-147.
Currency: 30, 74, 104, 108, 138-141, 143-145, 147, 183.
Custodianship: 66.

D

Debt: 6, 14-15, 20, 28, 32, 35, 38-46, 50, 54, 56-57, 60, 74, 77, 92, 104-106, 112, 115, 120, 122, 124-127, 140-142, 163-164, 172-173, 180, 184.
Debt free: 38.
Deceptions (of wealth): 68-75.
Deflation: 140-141.
Depression (financial): 141.
Disaster preparation: 103, 134, 149.
Discretionary expenses: 35.
Discipline (financial): 11, 14, 36-37, 41, 46, 48, 144, 184.
Disposable income: 9, 54, 169.
Diversification: 102-104, 106-108, 111, 113, 118, 120, 130, 143, 148.
Dividends: 14, 118, 143.
Divorce: 49.

E

Education: 6, 15, 44-45, 92, 122-125, 127, 130, 135, 140.
Emergency fund: 48, 50, 121-122, 132, 148-149.
Emergency preparations: 134.
Encouragement: 28, 45, 156.
Estate planning: 136-137.
Evangelism: 53, 88, 176-181.
ETFs: 117-118, 120, 141-142, 146.
Exercise: 37, 41, 67, 97, 136.
Expenses: 32, 35, 43, 46-50, 91-92, 111, 123, 129, 163.

F

Failure: 9-10, 40, 53, 69-70, 109, 139-140, 149.
Faith: 6-7, 10, 18, 21-22, 25-28, 31-33, 39, 41, 53, 56-58, 62, 72, 74, 80, 86, 89, 96-97, 153-154, 156, 158, 160-161, 169, 177, 179, 184.
Famine: 21, 41, 87, 104.
Federal Reserve: 21, 41, 87, 104.
FDIC (Federal Deposit Insurance Corporation): 104, 121, 141.
Fiduciary: 66.
Financial advisors: 112.
Fine art: 138.
Firstfruits: 16-17, 19, 22-23.

Food: 18, 25, 34-35, 38, 46-48, 55, 70-71, 73, 78, 91, 92, 106-107, 110, 135, 140, 160.
Fundamental analysis: 119.
Freedom: 6, 54, 55-56, 63, 89.

G

Gambler's ruin: 131.
Generosity: 12, 27, 58, 61-62, 70, 93, 132, 154, 157-158, 166, 169, 173, 179-180, 182-184.
Globalization: 74, 92.
Giving: 11, 16-17, 19-23, 25-33, 47, 58, 62, 65, 67, 77, 81, 84, 89, 151, 153-156, 159, 161-162, 164-166, 168-169, 171, 173-175, 178-179, 183, 184.
Gold: 63-67, 69, 71, 74, 102, 112, 144-146.
Good debt: 44-45, 54.
Grace: 19, 86, 87, 154, 156, 162, 169.
Graduate school: 126-127.
Greed: 27, 42, 55, 59-61, 71-72, 75, 87, 110, 120, 137, 155, 159-160, 166.
Growth: 8, 11, 31, 69, 76, 81, 125, 144, 179, 183-184.

H

Happiness: 10, 64, 71-72, 76, 184.
Hard work: 9, 82, 87-88, 108-111, 115, 125, 155.
Heart: 6-7, 12, 14, 16-22, 26-27, 30-31, 33, 40, 58-59, 61-62, 67, 69-70, 74-76, 80, 84, 86-87, 95-96, 151, 153, 155-156, 159, 160, 161-166, 170, 173, 181-184.
Health: 9, 47, 58, 135.
Health insurance: 31, 92, 107, 134, 136, 137, 140, 148.
Hedonic treadmill: 72.
Heavenly reward: 156.
Home ownership: 127.
Honoring God: 26-27, 33, 53, 62, 153, 157, 163.
Housing: 92, 113-114, 128-129, 131, 149.
Humility: 40, 157.
Hyperinflation: 139-141, 145.

I

Idolatry: 59, 159.
Income: 9, 20, 27, 33, 35, 43, 47, 49, 54, 61-62, 108, 110-111, 115, 122, 125, 127, 129, 134, 148, 162-163, 169, 179.
Inflation: 47, 92, 107, 121, 128, 130, 133, 139-141, 144, 145, 147-149.
Instrinct: 34, 49, 71-72, 120, 153.
Interest: 8, 14, 32, 38, 43-45, 54, 65-65, 81, 81, 104, 121, 127-130, 132, 138, 141, 163.
Investing: 11, 14, 43, 45, 48, 54, 56-58, 65-66, 97, 106-109, 111-112, 117, 120, 124-125, 131, 133, 143, 168, 179-180.

Investment property: 132.
Investor profile: 114-115.
IRA/Roth IRA: 48, 121-122, 148.

J

Joy: 21, 40, 45, 72, 75, 93, 95, 97, 156, 158, 161.

L

Law (of Moses): 22-23, 25.
Laziness: 40.
Lending: 10-11, 168.
Liquidity: 117, 132, 148.
Loans: 43-44, 92, 124, 129, 141.
Lottery:15, 35, 36, 72-73, 151.
Luxury: 36, 44.

M

Mammon: 59, 60, 68, 159, 169.
Marriage: 49-50.
Materialism: 20, 40, 60.
Medicare: 105.
Middle-class: 60.
Miracles: 55.
Missions work: 177, 183.
Money: 6, 8, 10-11, 14, 29-30, 32, 35-36, 39-41, 43-50, 53-58, 61, 64, 66, 68-70, 72, 74-77, 89-91, 93, 97, 103, 105, 107-108, 110-112, 114, 118, 120-122, 126-128, 130-134, 137, 139-141, 143-146, 148, 151-152, 155-157, 160-163, 165, 172, 177, 180-184, 191-195, 197-198.
Mutual funds: 106, 113, 117-118, 120, 141-142, 148.

N

(the) Needy: 58, 62, 161, 164-165, 172-175.
Normalcy bias: 149.
Non-correlated assets: 108.
Non-discretionary expenses: 35.

P

Patience: 14, 107, 111.
Pensions: 104-105, 122.
Personal finance: 4, 10-11, 14-15, 28, 162.
Personalities: 35.
(the) Poor: 19, 22, 36, 49, 54, 56, 62, 68-69, 73, 77, 82-86, 93, 108, 132, 137, 158, 161-162, 164, 168, 172-174, 175.

Prayer: 16, 18, 95, 165.
Preaching: 66, 176-178.
Precious metals: 138, 145, 146.
Prejudice: 86.
Preparation (for disaster): 103, 134, 149.
Pride: 40, 60, 69, 71, 160.
Prosperity gospel—health and wealth gospel: 80-81.

Q
Quantitative easing (a.k.a. QE): 92.

R
Real estate: 102, 106, 108, 133, 148.
Rebuke: 41-42.
Rental property: 132-133.
Retirement: 35, 46, 67, 104-105, 107, 115, 119, 121-122, 149, 163.
Reward in heaven: 56, 157-158, 175.
Rich: 9, 19, 36, 54-55, 60-61, 68, 70, 73, 77-78, 82-86, 89, 96, 110-111, 120, 132, 151, 156-158, 160, 162, 168, 180.
Richness toward God: 155.
Righteousness: 24, 37, 77, 79-81, 88-90, 97, 154, 164, 166.
Risk: 31, 43, 48-49, 82, 96-97, 102, 106-108, 115, 118, 120-121, 129-131, 133-134, 138-149, 158, 163.

S
Safety: 34, 70, 115, 144.
Salvation: 51, 75, 86-87, 176, 184.
Saving: 8-9, 29-30, 35, 46-48, 50, 89, 108, 11-112, 121-122, 129-132, 135, 141, 145, 179.
Schemes: 55, 110.
Self-righteousness: 164, 166.
Shrewdness: 138.
Sin: 16, 19, 23, 28, 40, 70, 75, 86, 90, 154, 165, 173, 178.
Silver: 60, 63, 69, 74, 145.
Slavery (debt): 44, 55-56, 74, 80, 172.
Sluggard: 46.
Social security: 30, 105.
Spending: 14, 29, 32, 34-36, 39-40, 46, 50, 56, 77, 88, 112, 140, 143, 161, 183.
Stinginess: 58, 164.
Stock market: 107-108, 113, 117, 141.
Stocks: 106, 108, 113, 115, 117-118, 120-121, 132, 140-141, 144, 148.
Stress: 35, 40, 45, 47, 49-50, 95, 125, 140.
Students: 38, 124, 127.

Surety: 43.

T
Talent(s): 9, 65, 66.
Taxes: 21, 23, 31, 38, 61, 104, 115, 128, 130, 133, 136, 147, 162.
Technical analysis: 119.
Time (as a resource or commodity): 14, 19, 30-33, 39-40, 44, 46, 56, 59, 62-63, 68, 70-72, 77, 88-89, 95-96, 103-104, 107, 112, 114, 115, 117, 119-121, 124-126, 128-130, 132-133, 135-137, 140, 143, 147, 151, 154, 162-163, 168-169, 171-172, 178-179, 183.
Time horizon: 115.
Tithe: 20-26, 29.
Treasure (in heaven): 58, 83, 96, 157, 183.

U
Unfunded liabilities: 106, 143.
Unity: 49-50.

V
Value: 30, 46, 49, 62, 74, 82, 88, 118, 121, 125-130, 139, 141, 145-148, 181.
Vision (for your life): 12, 97, 117, 181, 184.

W
Wall Street: 113-114, 117, 119-120, 124.
Wages: 69, 92.
Wealth: 6, 8-12, 14-16, 19, 22, 26, 30, 33-34, 36, 46, 50, 53-57, 59-80, 82-89, 91-92, 96, 99, 104, 106-107, 109, 111-113, 119, 124, 127, 131-134, 136-137, 144-145, 151-155, 157-160, 163-164, 166, 169, 180.
Wisdom: 6-8, 15, 23, 28-29, 55, 57, 68-70, 72, 76, 119, 125, 127, 182.
Works salvation: 86.
Worry: 91, 93-97, 126, 166.

Acknowledgments

How I ended up writing this book is both mysterious and amazing to me. God uses everything, including weakness and hardship, to accomplish his good purposes. His wisdom is deep, and his paths are beyond tracing out (Romans 11:33)!

I'm grateful that my beloved wife, Audrey Blair, has chosen to ride this rollercoaster called life with me. This book would not be possible without her love and wholehearted support. Even when I don't have confidence in myself, she always believes in me.

My mother, Sookja Blair, worked very hard while raising me and at the same time cared enough to push me toward excellence and achievement. Her love and support continue to this very day.

Greg Garcia first inspired me on the subject of the biblical handling of money with a seminar he gave in Los Angeles in 2002. Greg's efforts have changed my life and helped many others over the years.

My dear friend Bryan Ferguson was there to provide lots of encouragement and support throughout the process of writing this book. More importantly, he was there many years ago to show me the Scriptures, befriend me, and help save my soul.

Doug Jacoby and Gordon Ferguson both provided editing help at different stages of the writing of this book. I am grateful to both for their help, their faith, and their writings. I needed the admonishment, encouragement and assistance they provided.

Randy Jordan gave me important advice and encouragement when I first decided to write this book. The Honorable Kris Bailey gave me thoughtful feedback and encouragement on Chapter 1 of this book, which was very challenging to write. My good buddy Jerry Snow was there throughout with stimulating conversation, feedback and encouragement.

I also wanted to thank Dahle Bulosan, Dave Peickert, Dave Kim, Ramon Cordero, Greg and Ayesha Hankins, Kenny and Kaleah Batch, Janice Taylor, Don Norman, Tim Blake, Dominic Codispot, Matt Crisci, Josh Hendry, Jeff Spangler, Shelby Drabot, and Myiah Gauntlett for their support. Thanks to many in my church, including the now expired PTC Dead Prophets Society. Thanks to all my other family and friends who have supported me and made this book possible.

Thank you to Toney Mulhollan, Kiernan Antares, and the staff at Illumination Publishers. Lastly, I want to thank you, the reader, for looking into how you can better follow Jesus Christ in this area of your life.

—Patrick Blair 2019

Endnotes

1. This is commonly referred to as an exegesis, where one attempts to draw out the meaning rather than reading in his or her meaning. Of course, no one is unbiased and above introducing their own ideas into Scripture. Moreover, I've applied the Scriptures to many current issues of my choosing, which relies on my flawed human judgment.

2. Clason, George S. *The Richest Man in Babylon.* Place of Publication Not Identified: Dauphin Publications, 2017.

3. Morley, Brian K. "Tithe, Tithing—Baker's Evangelical Dictionary of Biblical Theology Online." Bible Study Tools. Accessed July 07, 2018. https://www.biblestudytools.com/dictionaries/bakers-evangelical-dictionary/tithe-tithing.html. "It is possible that there was only one tithe and that the differences in descriptions were due to changing circumstances. Numbers, written during the period of wandering, instructs the people to give their tithes to the Levites. Deuteronomy, written as Israel entered the land and began a more settled existence, required that tithes be eaten in the sanctuary (where the remaining portion was no doubt left). It seems every third year the tithe was given to the poor."

4. Service, Katherine Burgess, Religion News. "Report: Church Giving Reaches Depression-era Record Lows." The Washington Post. October 24, 2013. Accessed July 15, 2018. https://www.washingtonpost.com/national/on-faith/report-church-giving-reaches-depression-era-record-lows/2013/10/24/b2721a56-3ce9-11e3-b0e7-716179a2c2c7_story.html?noredirect=on&utm_term=.136890b5ba06. The statistic cited was from the Empty Tomb, Inc.'s report: *The State of Church Giving Through 2011.* While this statistic highlighted the drop in giving after the great recession, it gives the reader an idea of average church giving. Note also that the study did not include Catholics, but previous studies have shown Catholic giving to be very similar.

5. You can see here what I believe about how God created the world. Whatever you believe on this issue, I doubt it has any bearing on how you handle money.

6. Lin, Judy T., Christopher Bumcrot, Tippy Ulicny, Annamaria Lusardi, Gary Mottola, Christine Kieffer, and Gerri Walsh. *Financial Capability in the United States 2016.* Report. FINRA Foundation. 6. Accessed July 7, 2018. http://www.usfinancialcapability.org/downloads/NFCS_2015_Report_Natl_Findings.pdf.

7. Torre, Pablo S. "How (and Why) Athletes Go Broke." *Sports Illustrated*, March 23, 2009. Accessed July 7, 2018. https://www.si.com/vault/2009/03/23/105789480/how-and-why-athletes-go-broke.

8. *Robots.* Directed by Chris Wedge. Performed by Greg Kinnear and Robin Williams. United States: Blue Sky Studios, 2005. Film.

9. Franck, Thomas. "Debt for US Corporations Tops $6 Trillion." CNBC. June 27, 2018. Accessed July 7, 2018. https://www.cnbc.com/2018/06/27/debt-for-us-corporations-tops-6-trillion-sp-global.html.

Endnotes

10. "Compound Interest - Albert Einstein." Quotes on Finance. Accessed July 22, 2018. https://quotesonfinance.com/quote/79/albert-einstein-compound-interest.

11. Dickler, Jessica. "Credit Card Debt Hits a Record High. It's Time to Make a Payoff Plan." CNBC. January 23, 2018. Accessed July 7, 2018. https://www.cnbc.com/2018/01/23/credit-card-debt-hits-record-high.html.

12. "A Look at the Shocking Student Loan Debt Statistics for 2018." Student Loan Hero. May 1, 2018. Accessed July 7, 2018. https://studentloanhero.com/student-loan-debt-statistics/.

13. Lally, Tammy. "Money Shame." The Money Coach. Accessed March 02, 2019. https://tammylally.com/money-shame/.

14. *A Christmas Carol [Scrooge]*. Directed by Brian Desmond Hurst. By Noel Langley. Performed by Alistair Sim, Kathleen Harrison, and Mervyn Johns.

15. Tolstoy, Leo, and Leo Wiener. *The Complete Works of Count Tolstoy*. Vol. 17. Boston: D. Estes & Company, 1904. page 164.

16. *Report on the Economic Well-Being of U.S. Households in 2017*. Report. Board of Governors of the Federal Reserve System. May 22, 2018. 2. Accessed July 7, 2018.

17. Bell, Matt. "Tough Times Call for a Return to the Basics of Wise Money Management." Matt About Money. December 21, 2008. 1-2. Accessed July 7, 2018. https://www.mattaboutmoney.com/uploads/Financial-Stress.pdf.

18. I'm only using the concept of a slave in the same way the Bible is using it. I apologize in advance if this is offensive to anyone. Solomon was likely referring to literal debt slavery, where the borrower could become a physical slave to a creditor if a debt couldn't be repaid in a timely manner. Such practices have continued right up until modern times. Although debt slavery or debtor's prison may be illegal in your country, I don't believe it diminishes the meaning or power of this Scripture. However you look at it, when you owe, you owe and it's off to work you go!

19. "Mammon, n." OED Online. Oxford University Press, June 2016. Web. 3 September 2016.

20. Palus, Shannon. "Nine Out of Ten Americans Consider Themselves Middle Class." Smithsonian Institution. April 13, 2015. Accessed July 7, 2018. https://www.smithsonianmag.com/smart-news/nine-out-10-americans-consider-themselves-middle-class-180954970/.

21. The book of Luke also contains the Parable of the Minas (Luke 19:11-27), which is very similar.

22. "Talent (measurement)." Wikipedia. June 21, 2018. Accessed July 7, 2018. https://en.wikipedia.org/wiki/Talent_(measurement).

23. "Attribution Bias." Wikipedia. October 23, 2017. Accessed July 7, 2018. https://en.wikipedia.org/wiki/Attribution_bias#Self-serving_bias.

24. Jebb, Andrew T., Louis Tay, Ed Diener, and Shigehiro Oishi. "Happiness, Income Satiation and Turning Points around the World." *Nature Human Behavior*, January 2018, 33-38.

25. Robb, Simon. "Britain's Youngest Euromillions Winner Wants to Sue Lotto for 'ruining Her Life' Read More: Https://metro.co.uk/2017/02/12/britains-youngest-euromillions-winner-wants-to-sue-lotto-for-ruining-her-life-6442874. Metro UK. February 12, 2017. Accessed July 7, 2018. https://metro.co.uk/2017/02/12/britains-youngest-euromillions-winner-wants-to-sue-lotto-for-ruining-her-life-6442874/.

26. Hood, Neil. *Gods Wealth: Whose Money Is It Anyway?* Carlisle, Eng.: Authentic Lifestyle, 2004. 39.

27. "Prosperity Theology." Wikipedia. July 05, 2018. Accessed July 7, 2018. https://www.wikipedia.org/.

28. Richards, E. Randolph, and Brandon J. OBrien. *Misreading Scripture with Western Eyes: Removing Cultural Blinders to Better Understand the Bible.* Downers Grove, IL: InterVarsity Press, 2012. 192-193, 199-200. Similarly, Romans 8:28 is also commonly misread.

29. Randolph and Obrien, p. 41.

30. GotQuestions.org. "What Did Jesus Mean When He Said It Is Easier for a Camel to Go through the Eye of a Needle than for a Rich Man to Get into Heaven?" GotQuestions.org. February 21, 2018. Accessed July 07, 2018. https://www.gotquestions.org/camel-eye-needle.html.

31. I have never had bitterness or disdain for my former boss. He was merely calling me to the lifestyle he was living at the time.

32. Goldberg, H., & Lewis, R.T. (1978). Money madness: The psychology of saving, spending, loving, and hating money. New York: William Morrow and Company, Inc. 14.

33. Miller, David W. "Wealth Creation as Integrated with Faith: A Protestant Reflection" Muslim, Christian, and Jewish Views on the Creation of Wealth April 23–24, 2007.

34. I really like this quote: "Who has time? Who has time? But then if we do not ever take time, how can we ever have time?" Merovingian, The Matrix Reloaded. In today's busy world, making time for God, family, and yourself takes a conscious and deliberate decision.

35. Based on the U.S. Department of Labor, Bureau of Labor Statistics CPI Inflation Calculator (https://www.bls.gov/data/inflation_calculator.htm).

36. Hathaway, Terry, and Lao Tzu. The Old Man and His Horse. Accessed February 28, 2019. https://www.hathaworld.com/aware/short/horseman.htm. The story from the website has been abbreviated and altered for stylistic reasons. There are many differing versions of this story online.

37. Attributed to author and financial commentator Jim Rickards.

38. Keep in mind that the S&P 500 charts do not account for inflation and do not represent the same stocks over time. The S&P 500 is an index of the 500 U.S. stocks with the largest market capitalization. In other words, when an S&P 500 stock is no longer performing as well and loses market capitalization, it can fall out of the index and another stock replaces it. It is important not to misunderstand indexes and other statistics.

39. Staff, Investopedia. "Diversification." Investopedia. June 25, 2018. Accessed July 07, 2018. https://www.investopedia.com/terms/d/diversification.asp.

40. "Diversification (finance)." Wikipedia. July 03, 2018. Accessed July 07, 2018. https://en.wikipedia.org/wiki/Diversification_(finance).

41. Shakespeare, William, Jonathan Bate, and Eric Rasmussen. *The Merchant of Venice*. New York: Modern Library, 2010.

42. The New Living Translation for verse 2 is: "But divide your investments among many places, for you do not know what risks might lie ahead."

43. Some commentators believe Ecclesiastes 11:1-2 refers to placing seed grain in wet areas (e.g. near a river bank), in hopes there may be some harvest when the water recedes. This being a metaphor for giving food to the poor in that the act is akin to wasting the seed (bread). In other words, be charitable even though it may not seem to benefit you and God will ultimately take care of you. Although I don't completely disagree with the sentiment, I find this interpretation to be far too problematic. I believe my interpretation of the passage to be consistent with Solomon's character, other writings, and the fact that he had a lot of success with international trade (1 Kings 10:22-29).

44. Delevingne, Lawrence. "Outlook for Pensions Is Pretty Awful: Bridgewater." CNBC. April 16, 2014. Accessed July 07, 2018. https://www.cnbc.com/2014/04/15/controversial-bridgewater-report-says-most-pensions-could-fail.html.

45. Woolley, Suzanne. "Retirement Dread Is Replacing the American Dream." Retirement Dread Is Replacing the American Dream. July 18, 2017. Accessed July 07, 2018. https://www.msn.com/en-us/money/retirement/retirement-dread-is-replacing-the-american-dream/ar-BBEFPuq?li=BBnbfcN.

46. Pear, Robert. "Medicare's Trust Fund Is Set to Run Out in 8 Years. Social Security, 16." The New York Times. June 05, 2018. Accessed July 07, 2018. https://www.nytimes.com/2018/06/05/us/politics/medicare-social-security-finances.html.

47. Prior to World War II, the United States and much of the world was struggling with the after effects of the 1929 Crash and the ensuing Great Depression, which lasted from 1929-1941.

48. U.S. Department of the Treasury. Fiscal Service, Federal Debt: Total Public Debt [GFDEBTN], retrieved from FRED, Federal Reserve Bank of St. Louis; https://fred.stlouisfed.org/series/GFDEBTN, July 5, 2018.

49. "U.S. National Debt Clock: Real Time." US Debt Clock.org. Accessed March 05, 2019. http://www.usdebtclock.org/.

50. See http://demonocracy.info/infographics/usa/us_debt/us_debt.html to help you visualize large amounts of cash and debt.

51. Staff, NPR. "Any Way You Stack It, $14.3 Trillion Is A Mind-Bender." NPR. June 04, 2011. Accessed July 07, 2018. https://www.npr.org/2011/06/04/136930966/how-much-is-14-3-trillion-it-s-a-brain-teaser.

52. Katz, Robert W. *The Solomon Portfolio: How to Invest like a King*. Sanford, FL: DC Press, 2009.

53. Clason, George S. *The Richest Man in Babylon.* Place of Publication Not Identified: Dauphin Publications, 2017.

54. Attributed to ancient Greek philosopher Heraclitus (paraphrase).

55. "Dow Jones - 100 Year Historical Chart." MacroTrends. Accessed July 07, 2018. http://www.macrotrends.net/1319/dow-jones-100-year-historical-chart.

56. Attributed to U.S. author William A. Feather.

57. Personally, I have no professional expertise and have experienced mixed results. I am neither encouraging nor discouraging anyone from being invested in stock markets.

58. Attributed to Scottish economist, philosopher, and author Adam Smith.

59. This psychological dynamic affects both short-term traders and long-term investors alike.

60. Attributed to U.S. businessman and President Donald J. Trump.

61. Attributed to U.S. investor Warren Buffet.

62. Attributed to English physicist and philosopher Sir Isaac Newton.

63. See this web page for a good overview of the differences between the federal Coverdell plan and state 529 plans: "Coverdell Education Savings Account." Wikipedia. January 14, 2018. Accessed July 07, 2018. https://en.wikipedia.org/wiki/Coverdell_Education_Savings_Account.

64. By no means is the value of education limited to traditional degree programs.

65. "Lifetime Earnings by Degree Type." The Hamilton Project. Accessed July 09, 2018. http://www.hamiltonproject.org/charts/lifetime_earnings_by_degree_type.

66. "U.S. Student Loan Debt Statistics for 2018." Student Loan Hero. Accessed July 09, 2018. https://studentloanhero.com/student-loan-debt-statistics/. The statement is based on U.S. Census data interpreted by Hershbein and Kearney in 2014.

67. "U.S. National Debt Clock: Real Time." US Debt Clock.org. Accessed July 07, 2018. http://www.usdebtclock.org/.

68. Board of Governors of the Federal Reserve System (US), Student Loans Owned and Securitized, Outstanding [SLOAS], retrieved from FRED, Federal Reserve Bank of St. Louis; https://fred.stlouisfed.org/series/SLOAS, July 6, 2018.

69. i.e. Correlation does not equal causation.

70. Graf, Nikki, Richard Fry, and Cary Funk. "7 Facts about the STEM Workforce." Pew Research Center. January 09, 2018. Accessed July 09, 2018. http://www.pewresearch.org/fact-tank/2018/01/09/7-facts-about-the-stem-workforce/.

71. Early in our marriage, my wife and I argued about this subject a lot. I tended to look at higher education only as a means to an end. I learned from her to appreciate the value of the accomplishment itself.

72. I also realize that many people reading this will be in a position to guide their children and grandchildren in this regard.

73. I realize that a truly high level of prestige can pay dividends in some cases and may be worth the cost (e.g. Harvard, Yale, Stanford).

74. It makes a huge difference when a family can help pay for college or professional school. It is no surprise that most people who go to professional schools come from wealthy families. Whether your family is wealthy or not, be grateful if your family helps you through school!

75. Clifford, Catherine. "29-year-old CEO Who Manages $1 Billion Warns Young People: Buying a Home Can Be a 'terrible Investment'." CNBC. July 21, 2017. Accessed July 09, 2018. https://www.cnbc.com/2017/07/21/ceo-michael-katchen-says-buying-a-home-can-be-a-terrible-investment.html.

76. US Census Bureau. "Census.gov." Census Bureau QuickFacts. Accessed March 07, 2019. https://www.census.gov/const/uspriceann.pdf.

77. "Average & Median Sale Price for A New Home." Average and Median Cost for A Pre-owned (Used) Home in The United States. Accessed July 09, 2018. http://www.fedprimerate.com/new_home_sales_price_history.htm#preliminarydata.

78. My favorite housing bust term is "NINJA loan": no income, no job, no asset loans. It's ridiculous that a bank would loan hundreds of thousands of dollars to someone without any evidence that the person might repay the loan. It's hard to believe, but NINJA loans were really given out.

79. However, there's not usually much net upside if you buy again. This works best for those who downsize or shift to renting.

80. "Gambler's Ruin." 2018. Wikipedia. Wikimedia Foundation. July 3. https://en.wikipedia.org/wiki/Gambler's_ruin.

81. ONeill, Eugene, and Ferdinand Schunck. 2016. *Long Days Journey into Night*. Stuttgart: Reclam.

82. Kiyosaki, Robert T. 2017. *Rich Dad Poor Dad: What the Rich Teach Their Kids About Money That the Poor and Middle Class Do Not!* Perseus Distribution Services.

83. For owners of large or numerous rental properties, the dynamic changes, because it becomes your business, where you might hire managers or property management companies to handle your affairs.

84. "Are You Ready? Why Prepare?" July 26, 2013. FEMA. https://www.fema.gov/media-library-data/20130726-1549-20490-4325/why_prepare.pdf.

85. Rose, Charlie. 2017. FEMA administrator: "Long way to go" to create a culture of preparedness. Other. *CBS This Morning*. CBS.

86. Staff, Investopedia. 2018. "Counterparty Risk." *Investopedia*. Investopedia. June 27. https://www.investopedia.com/terms/c/counterpartyrisk.asp.

87. See, e.g., A.M. Best Rating Services.

88. Delgado, Antonio Maria. 2018. "In Venezuela, Inflation Quadruples to 18,000 Percent in Two Months, with No End in Sight." *Miamiherald*. Miami Herald. May 2. http://www.miamiherald.com/news/nation-world/world/americas/venezuela/article210282264.html.

89. Bernholz, Peter. *Monetary Regimes and Inflation: History, Economic and*

Political Relationships. Cheltenham: Edward Elgar, 2006, Chapter 5.3.

90. "Powell: We're Not on a Fiscally Sustainable Path." Interview by Rep. Bruce Poliquin. CNBC. February 2, 2018. Accessed July 11, 2018. https://www.cnbc.com/video/2018/02/27/powell-were-not-on-a-sustainable-fiscal-path.html.

91. Which snowflake causes the avalanche? Which straw breaks the camel's back? It's impossible to know and doesn't really matter.

92. See e.g., Larrick, Bart De LangheStefano PuntoniRichard. "Linear Thinking in a Nonlinear World." Harvard Business Review. July 18, 2017. Accessed July 11, 2018. https://hbr.org/2017/05/linear-thinking-in-a-nonlinear-world.

93. Polgar, Andrei. *The Age of Anomaly: Spotting Financial Storms in a Sea of Uncertainty*. North Charleston, SC: CreateSpace Independent Publishing Platform, 2018. After reading this book, I realized that some readers of my book will need a message to balance out their approach.

94. Rickards, James. *The New Case for Gold*. London: Portfolio Penguin, 2016, 4.

95. Rand, Ayn, Nathaniel Branden, Alan Greenspan, and Robert Hessen. *Capitalism: The Unknown Ideal*. New York: Signet, 2008 ("Gold and Economic Freedom," 1967 by Alan Greenspan).

96. Also, the stores of above-ground silver are relatively small, because silver is used and disposed of in a way that either cannot be recovered or is not cost-effective to recover. In contrast, nearly all the gold ever mined in history is still in a tradeable form today.

97. Stevenson, Abigail. "Cramer: How Much Gold to Have in Your Portfolio." CNBC. March 03, 2016. Accessed July 11, 2018. https://www.cnbc.com/2016/03/03/cramer-best-insurance-policy-for-your-portfolio.html.

98. Gresham's law states that "bad money drives out good," which is an explanation of why gold and silver are out of circulation. The theory is that people will spend the "bad" money and keep the "good" money, when the current law makes all the money have equal value. Staff, Investopedia. "Gresham's Law." Investopedia. April 10, 2018. Accessed July 24, 2018. https://www.investopedia.com/terms/g/greshams-law.asp.

99. Investopedia. "Cryptocurrency." Investopedia. July 05, 2018. Accessed July 11, 2018. https://www.investopedia.com/terms/c/cryptocurrency.asp.

100. Ironically, the limitation on the number of Bitcoins tends to be deflationary as more people use them. Among other technological challenges, its deflationary nature is a real impediment to using Bitcoin as a medium of exchange.

101. "Normalcy Bias." Wikipedia. July 03, 2018. Accessed July 11, 2018. https://en.wikipedia.org/wiki/Normalcy_bias.

102. Lewis, C. S. *God in the Dock*.

103. Wood, Graeme. "Secret Fears of the Super-Rich." The Atlantic. August 25, 2015. Accessed July 11, 2018. https://www.theatlantic.com/magazine/archive/2011/04/secret-fears-of-the-super-rich/308419/.

104. Keep in mind that being rich toward God alone does not mean that you've mastered mammon. We are continually called to trust God throughout our lives. We must keep our hearts from loving money and falling victim to its inherent

Endnotes

dangers (see Chapters 6-8).

105. Notable people such as Bill Gates and Warren Buffet have made the pledge. See https://givingpledge.org/About.aspx for information.

106. This isn't only a result of a mind change regarding the needs of others, but also has a lot to do with me getting my own act together financially. When you have bad debt and are insecure financially, it makes giving feel more burdensome.

107. Kinnard, Dr. G. Steve. *Jesus and the Poor.* Spring, TX: Illumination Publishers, 2017, 26.

108. Sider, Ronald J. *Rich Christians in an Age of Hunger: Moving from Affluence to Generosity.* 6th ed. Nashville, TN: W Publishing Group, an Imprint of Thomas Nelson, 2015.

109. Sider, p. 36.

110. Sider, p. 37.

111. Campbell, Alexia Fernández. "Why Are Americans Less Charitable Than They Used to Be?" The Atlantic. December 27, 2016. Accessed July 11, 2018. https://www.theatlantic.com/business/archive/2016/12/americans-donate-less-to-charity/511397/.

112. Sider, p. 198 (fn 36, p. 323).

113. Sider, p. 199 (quoting the Economist, May 5, 2001, 59-62; see also, Carbaugh, International Economist, 59.

114. Sider p. 198-199.

115. Compare this with the apostle Paul's planned collections for churches elsewhere. There's nothing wrong with giving in a calculated way.

116. See also Psalm 112:5 and Luke 14:12-14.

117. "We Are the World" by Lionel Richie, Stevie Wonder, Paul Simon, Kenny Rogers, James Ingram, Tina Turner, Billy Joel, Michael Jackson, and many others (1985).

118. "Another Day in Paradise" by Phil Collins (1989).

119. "Praying for Time" by George Michael (1990).

120. "Luke 16:9 - Welcomed Into Eternal Dwellings - Wisconsin Evangelical Lutheran Synod (WELS)." EveryCRSReport.com. Accessed July 11, 2018. https://wayback.archive-it.org/all/20090927182708/https://www.wels.net/cgi-bin/site.pl?1518&cuTopic_topicID=813&cuItem_itemID=17890.

121. By no means should physically serving one another in church enable laziness or freeloading (2 Thessalonians 3:10). Anyone who receives help should also be doing their best and humbly accepting input on how to better their own situation. Also, the burden of service should be shared by all in the church (1 Corinthians 12:26).

122. C. Bartholomew and T. Mortiz, *Christ and Consumerism: A Critical Analysis of the Spirit of the Age* (Carlisle: Paternoster, 2000), p. 81. This series of essays provides thought-provoking insights into consumerism.

Faith and Finances Ministry
www.faith-finances.com

Thank you for taking the time to read Faith and Finances. If you want to look at more information, including helpful blog articles and resources, please visit the Faith and Finances Ministry at www.faith-finances.com.

Coming soon!

Faith and Finances Companion Study Guide
- In-depth personal exploration
- Practical application of biblical financial principles
- Help with budgeting, offerings, and investing
- Activities for small group meetings
- Church course materials included:
    - —Flexible course outlines to match your church's schedule
    - —No course fees or training fees
    - —No need for facilitators or training classes
    - —Create a culture of personal and congregational growth